First published in 2019 by Raspberry Pi Trading Ltd, Maurice Wilkes Building,
St. John's Innovation Park, Cowley Road, Cambridge, CB4 0DS

Publishing Director: Russell Barnes • Editor: Phil King • Sub Editor: Nicola King
Author: Simon Long • Design: Critical Media
CEO: Eben Upton

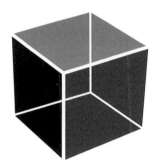

Welcome to
An Introduction to C
& GUI Programming

The C programming language was invented in the early 1970s, and since then has become one of the most popular and widely used general-purpose languages. C can be used to create simple command-line programs, or embedded code to operate the tiny microcontrollers in toasters and watches. At the other extreme, it can be used to create rich graphical desktop applications – in fact, most of Linux (and Raspberry Pi OS itself) is written in it. It can give you control over the smallest details of how a processor operates, but is still simple to learn and read. The first part of this book is an introduction to programming in C for absolute beginners; the second part shows how to use C to create desktop applications for Raspberry Pi OS. You don't need any programming experience, and a Raspberry Pi running Raspberry Pi OS is all you need to get started.

About the Author

Simon Long is an engineer working for Raspberry Pi. He is responsible for the Raspberry Pi Desktop and its associated applications. Before joining Raspberry Pi, he worked for Broadcom, where he first met Eben Upton, and before that spent ten years working as a software engineer and user interface designer for a major consultancy firm. In his spare time, he enjoys solving those really hard crosswords without any black squares.

"Dedicated to the memory of Pythagoras, a very special cat, and my devoted companion while writing this book."

Contents

Chapter 1
Getting started

C is one of the most widely used programming languages
– learn how to use it to program the Raspberry Pi!

What's so great about C?

C is a very versatile and widely used programming language. It has been used to write pretty much everything, from low-level routines to control the hardware in embedded microcontrollers to complete operating systems like Linux with graphical user interfaces. In spite of this huge flexibility, it is also relatively simple – the language only has about 20 or so keywords, but there are huge libraries of additional functions that you can call on when you need them. In the first part of this book, we are going to concentrate on learning about the keywords, with a few of the more commonly used library functions; the second part of the book shows how to use the GTK library to make it easy to write graphical interfaces in C.

Many of the languages that you may have seen, such as Python, are what are called *interpreted languages*. This means that the code you write is run directly: each line of code is read in and interpreted as you run it. C is different: it's a *compiled language*. This means that the code you write, known as the *source code*, is never run directly. The source code is passed through a program called a *compiler*, which converts it into a machine-readable version called an *executable* or a *binary*; you then run the resulting executable.

This may seem complex, but it has a few big advantages. First, it means that you don't need to have a copy of C itself on every computer you want to run your program on; once compiled, the executable is standalone and self-contained. Second, the compilation process will find a lot of errors before you even run the program (but it won't usually find all of them). Most importantly, the compilation process means that the time-consuming translation of human-readable code into machine-readable instructions has already happened, which means that compiled code generally runs many times faster than interpreted code would.

CHOOSE YOUR EDITOR

You can use whatever editor you like to enter code, as long as it saves it as plain text. The Geany editor included in Raspberry Pi OS is a good choice, but you can also use Leafpad, nano, or any others that you prefer.

> ## WHITESPACE DOESN'T MATTER!
>
> Unlike Python, whitespace has no significance in C – you can put spaces, tabs, and new lines anywhere you like in a C program to make it readable.

Hello world – your first C program

With all that out of the way – which has hopefully made you think that C might be worth learning – let's have a look at the first program everyone writes in any language, the one that prints 'Hello World' on the screen. Incidentally, the tradition of writing a Hello World program was first introduced with the original documentation describing C itself. Just think: no C, no Hello World...

```c
#include <stdio.h>

void main (void)
{
  /* A print statement */
  printf ("Hello world!\n");
}
```

Hopefully not too frightening! Let's look at it line by line.

```c
#include <stdio.h>
```

This is known as a *hash-include*. As mentioned above, the C language has a large library of functions that can be included, and we need to use one of them in this program: the formatted print command **printf**. This is part of the standard input-output library, or **stdio** for short. So what this line does is to warn the compiler that the program needs the **stdio** library to be included as part of the compile process.

```c
void main (void)
```

C is a function-based language; every program is made up of a number of functions.

Each function takes zero or more arguments, and returns a single value. A function definition consists of a specification of what the function returns (in this case, a **void**), a function name (in this case, **main**), and a list of arguments enclosed in round brackets (again, a **void**).

Every C program has to include a function called **main**; when you run the compiled program, the **main** function is the first thing that executes.

The word **void** is called a *type specifier*; a **void** is a special type which means 'no value required'. We'll look more at types in the next chapter.

So this line defines the **main** function for this program; it states that the **main** function takes no arguments, and returns no value.

The code which makes up the function itself is enclosed between the two curly brackets **{}** that follow the function definition.

```
/* A print statement */
```

First, we have a comment telling us what's going on. Comments in C start with the symbol **/***, and end with ***/** – anything between those two symbols is ignored by the compiler.

The code itself is just one line:

```
printf ("Hello world!\n");
```

This is a call to the **printf** ('print formatted') function from the **stdio** library. In this case, it takes a single argument, which is a text string enclosed within double quotes. As mentioned above, function arguments are enclosed in round brackets.

Note that the line ends with a semicolon. All statements in C must finish with a semicolon; this tells the compiler that this is the end of a statement. One of the most common beginner mistakes in C is to forget a semicolon somewhere!

What about the string itself? The **Hello World!** bit is straightforward enough, but what about that **\n** at the end? Remember this function is called 'print formatted'? Well, the **\n** is a bit of formatting; it's the symbol for a newline character. So this line will print the string 'Hello World!', followed by a new line.

CHECK YOUR BRACKETS

Unlike whitespace, punctuation is very important in C – make sure you don't use a curly bracket where a round one is needed, or vice versa.

Compiling your program

Let's compile and run this. Raspberry Pi OS includes a C compiler called gcc, so there's nothing to install; just start up Raspberry Pi OS on your Raspberry Pi and you're ready to go. Use your favourite text editor to create a file called **hello.c**, copy the program above into it, and save it. Then, from a terminal, go into the directory where you saved **hello.c** and enter:

```
gcc -o myprog hello.c
```

This calls the gcc C compiler with the option **-o myprog**, which tells it to create an executable output file called **myprog**, and to use **hello.c** as the input source code.

If you entered your C code correctly (did you make sure the semicolon was there?), this should take a second or so and then return you to the command line. There should now be a file in the current directory called **myprog** – try running it by typing:

```
./myprog
```

Et voilà! You should now have...

```
Hello World!
```

...written in the terminal.

▲ You interact with both the C compiler and your compiled C programs from the command line; you can either do this in a terminal window in the desktop, or by booting your Raspberry Pi straight to the command line

RUNNING YOUR PROGRAM

You need to tell Linux that the program you want to run is in the current directory, so don't forget the **./** before **myprog**, or it won't know where to look!

That's your first C program written, compiled, and run. In the next chapter, we'll start using C for something a bit more useful...

Chapter 2

Variables and arithmetic

Doing some real work in C: creating variables and performing mathematical operations on them

I
n some languages, you can create variables as you go along and put whatever data you want into them. C isn't like that: to use a variable in C, you need to have created it first, and at the time you create it, you have to set what type of value it's going to store. By doing this, a block of memory of the correct size can be allocated by the compiler to hold the variable. This process of creating a variable is known as *declaration*.

Integers

There are several fundamental data types in C, but we'll start by looking at one of the most commonly used: the **int** type, used to store an integer value.

```
#include <stdio.h>

void main (void)
{
  int a;
  int b = 3;
  int c;

  a = 2;
  c = a + b;
  printf ("The sum of adding %d and %d is %d\n", a, b, c);
}
```

The top three lines inside the **main** function here are declarations. They tell the compiler that we would like to use variables called **a**, **b**, and **c** respectively, and that each one is of type **int**, i.e. an integer.

In the second line, we see an example of an *initialisation* at the same time as a declaration: this stores an initial value of 3 in the variable **b**. Note that the values of **a** and **c** at this point are undefined; you might assume that a variable which hasn't had a value stored in it is always 0, but that isn't the case in C. Before reading the value from a variable or using it in a calculation, you must store a value in it; reading a variable before initialising it is a common error in C.

The next two lines do some actual work with the variables we have declared.

```
a = 2;
```

This stores a value of 2 in the variable **a**, which will now have this value until it's changed. The reason **a** is called a variable is that it can *vary*: you can change its value as often as you like, but only to another integer. The value of a variable can change, but its type is fixed when it is declared.

```
c = a + b;
```

This line adds **a** to **b**, and stores the result in **c**.

```
printf ("The sum of adding %d and %d is %d\n", a, b, c);
```

This is another use of the formatted print function we saw in the previous chapter. Note the three **%d** symbols inside the string: these are *format specifiers*, and they are how you output numbers in C. When the **printf** function is executed, each **%d** is replaced by a decimal representation (d for decimal integer) of the variable in the corresponding position in the list after the string. So the first **%d** will be replaced by the value of **a**, the second with the value of **b**, and the third with the value of **c**.

Compile the program above and then run it. You should see this in the terminal:

```
The sum of adding 2 and 3 is 5
```

MULTIPLE DECLARATIONS

You can declare multiple variables of the same type in one line, separated by commas.
For the example here, instead of three separate **int** declarations, you could type
`int a, b = 3, c;` on one line.

Floating-point numbers

So we can add two integers together; what else can we do? One thing we might want to do is to use floating-point numbers: numbers with a decimal point. These have a different type, called **float**. Try changing the code above so instead of:

```
int a;
```

...you have:

```
float a;
```

This tells the compiler that **a** is now a floating-point value, rather than an integer. Compile and run your program. What happens?

Oops! That doesn't look right, does it? What has happened is that, while the maths is still all correct, the **printf** statement is now wrong; you're telling it to print **a**, which is a floating-point value, as a decimal integer. To fix that, change the first **%d** in the **printf** function to **%f**, which is the format specifier for a floating-point number, like this:

```
printf ("The sum of adding %f and %d is %d\n", a, b, c);
```

That should produce something a lot more sensible when you run it. This is an important lesson about C: it will do exactly what you tell it to, even if it makes no sense. You told it to show you a floating-point number as if it were a decimal integer, and the compiler assumed that was what you wanted, even though the result was nonsense.

When you're working with variables, always keep track of what values you're putting in what types, as it's easy to introduce errors by assuming a variable is of one type when it's actually another. One common error is to put the results of a calculation on floating-point values into an integer.

Try this: make **b** a float as well (not forgetting to change its format specifier in the **printf**), but leave **c** as an int, and set the two floats to values with decimal points, like this:

```
float a;
float b = 3.641;
int c;

a = 2.897;
c = a + b;
printf ("The sum of adding %f and %f is %d\n", a, b, c);
```

You'll see a result like:

```
The sum of adding 2.897000 and 3.641000 is 6
```

6? That's not right! But it's exactly what you've asked for. What the compiler did was to add the two floating-point values together, and got the answer 6.538, but you then told the compiler to put that into **c**, an integer variable. So the compiler just threw away everything after the decimal point! If you change **c** to a float, and change the final **%d** to **%f**, you'll find it gives the correct answer.

ARITHMETIC SHORTHAND

C allows shortcuts for some common operations; for example, instead of typing **a = a + 1**, you can just enter **a++**. Or for **a = a * 3**, you can enter **a *= 3**.

▾ Don't forget to use **%f** instead of **%d** as the print specifier when changing the int values to float values in the example

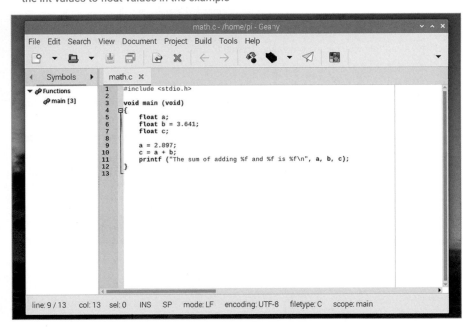

DECIMAL PLACES

You can set the number of decimal places to display for a floating-point type specifier in **printf** by putting a decimal point and the number of places between the **%** and the **f** – so **%.3f** will show a float value with three digits after the decimal point.

Other types

Another common variable type is **char**, a character value. This is used, as the name suggests, to store a single character. The ASCII character encoding uses a single value between 0 and 127 for each letter, number, and punctuation symbol, so a char is a single byte; it's really just an integer value which can only hold small numbers. The compiler allocates several bytes to store an int or a float, but only allocates a single byte of memory to store a char.

There are also modifiers which can be applied to variable types. Both **char** and **int** can be used to store both positive and negative numbers, but by applying the **unsigned** modifier when one is declared, they can be restricted to only store positive values. So...

```
char a;
```

...declares a variable which can hold values from -128 to 127, while...

```
unsigned char a;
```

...declares a variable which can hold values from 0 to 255.

When doing arithmetic with chars, it is important to make sure that the answers to any calculation will fit into the variable. If, say, you have a char containing the value 100, and you add 30 to it, you would expect to end up with the result 130 – but as above, a char can only hold values up to 127. So the value your char will actually end up containing is -126, because values over 127 – the highest value a char can store – wrap around to the lowest value (-128) and start counting up from there. This 'overflow' behaviour is a common cause of bugs in C programs which do arithmetic.

REMEMBER PRECEDENCE

C obeys the common rules for operator precedence – so **a = a + 2 * 3** evaluates the multiply first and then adds the result, 6, to **a**. You can use round brackets to change precedence – **a = (a + 2) * 3** gives 3a + 6.

That gives you some idea about how C handles numbers, and how you can use it for arithmetic; in the next chapter, we'll look at how to use the results of calculations to make decisions.

Chapter 3

Conditions and comparisons

Branches and loops: controlling the flow of your C program

O ne of the fundamentals of any programming language is the ability to make conditional operations – to change the program's flow depending on the result of a test.

In this chapter, we'll look at how you test conditions within your C programs, and how you use the results to determine what happens next.

In C, the mechanism for controlling flow based on testing a condition is the *if-else* statement. Here's a simple example:

```c
#include <stdio.h>

void main (void)
{
  int a = 0;

  if (a == 0)
  {
    printf ("a is equal to 0\n");
  }
  else
  {
    printf ("a is not equal to 0\n");
  }
}
```

Here, the keyword **if** is followed by a test enclosed in round brackets, in this case `(a == 0)`. If the test evaluates as true, the operations enclosed by the curly brackets after the test are executed.

This example also shows the use of an else clause. At the end of the curly brackets around the operations which you want to execute if the test is true, there's an **else** followed by another set of curly brackets; these contain the operations you want to execute if the original test evaluated as false.

Try compiling the code above, and change the value with which **a** is initialised to make sure it does what you expect.

= or ==

That's all fine, but what's this **a == 0** all about? Surely if we want to know whether a is equal to 0, we just put **a = 0**? Why the two equals signs? Well, try replacing the double equals sign with a single equals and see what happens.

This is a very important aspect of C syntax, and a common source of bugs. The equals sign is used for two different things: one is to assign a value to a variable, whereas the other is to test whether a variable is equal to a value. A single equals sign (=) *assigns* a variable; a double equals sign (==) *tests* a variable.

So the statement...

```
if (a == 0)
```

...tests to see if **a** is equal to 0. If it is, then the test evaluates as true, and the code immediately after the **if** is executed.

But the statement...

```
if (a = 0)
```

...doesn't compare **a** against 0 at all: it just sets **a** to 0. So how does the compiler decide what to do next? In this case, it just looks at the value of what's in the brackets; you've set **a** to 0, so the value inside the brackets is 0.

In C, a value of 0 is equivalent to false, and a non-zero value is equivalent to true. So by replacing the double equals with a single equals, you've changed the value of **a**, and then you look to see if the value you've set **a** to is equivalent to true or false; neither of which were what you wanted to do! If a C program is behaving strangely, check very carefully that all your tests are actually tests and not assignments: this is a very easy mistake to make.

So == is the test to see if a value is equal to another one. There are other useful symbols that can be used in a test. The symbol **!=**, for example, means 'is not equal to'.

The mathematical operators > and < are used to test for 'is greater than' and 'is less than' respectively, and they can also be combined with an equals sign to give >= and <=, the tests for 'is greater than or equal to' and 'is less than or equal to'.

You can combine tests with logical operators. The symbol **&&** is a Boolean AND (i.e. test whether both sides are true), and **||** is a Boolean OR (i.e. test if either side is true). So, to execute code only if both **a** and **b** are 0, you would use **if (a == 0 && b == 0)**. To test if either **a** or **b** is 0, you use **if (a == 0 || b == 0)**.

Similarly, you can use the operator **!** as a Boolean NOT to invert the result of a test, so **if (!(a == 0))** is the same as **if (a != 0)** .

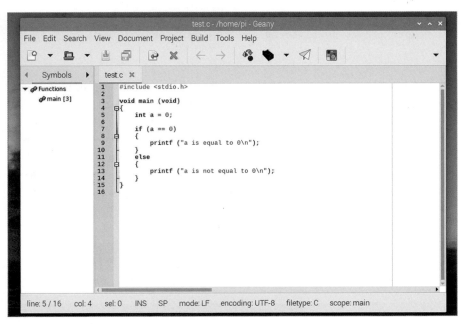

▲ Make sure that you use a double equals sign in the brackets after the if, not a single one!

ELSE-IF

You can have multiple else statements in one test. Instead of one simple else for one alternative, use `else if ()` with a new test for each alternative you want. We'll look more at this in the next chapter.

Looping

The if statement is useful for making a single decision, but what if you want to do something repeatedly until a test is true or false? We use a *while* loop for this, and here's an example:

```
#include <stdio.h>

void main (void)
{
  int a = 0;

  while (a < 5)
  {
    printf ("a is equal to %d\n", a);
    a++;
  }
  printf ("a is equal to %d and I've finished\n", a);
}
```

This is very similar to an if statement, but the code in the curly brackets is executed repeatedly for as long as the test in the round brackets is true, not just once.

So in our example code, **a** is initialised to 0. We enter the while loop, and test to see if **a** is less than 5, which it is, so the code inside the curly brackets is executed. The value of **a** is printed out, then we have one of C's useful shortcuts to save too much typing…

a++ is the same as **a=a+1**; the double plus means 'add one to this variable'. Similarly, **a--** means 'subtract one from this variable'; these are very commonly used to count the times around a loop. The notation **a+=1** can also be used to add a value to a variable; this also works for other arithmetic operators, so **a*=3** multiplies **a** by 3, and so on.

In the while loop, each time the code in the curly brackets has been executed, the test in the round brackets is repeated; if it's still true, the loop code is repeated again. As soon as the test is false, execution continues with the line after the closing curly bracket.

INFINITE LOOPS

Make sure your loops always finish! If the condition you test in a while loop never evaluates to false, your program will sit in the loop forever and never finish. If a program appears to be doing nothing when you run it, check your loop tests.

Sometimes, we might want a loop which always runs at least once before a test is made. We do this with a small modification to the syntax to create a *do-while* loop:

```
#include <stdio.h>

void main (void)
{
```

```
int a = 0;

do
{
  printf ("a is equal to %d\n", a);
  a++;
} while (a < 5);
printf ("a is equal to %d and I've finished\n", a);
}
```

The keyword **do** now goes before the curly bracket, and the **while** and test go after the closing curly bracket. When this runs, the code in the loop always executes once before the test; you can test this by running both the loop examples above with **a** initialised to 5 rather than 0, and seeing how the behaviour differs.

MORE ABOUT SEMICOLONS

Unlike the test in an if statement or a while loop, you need to put a semicolon after the test in a do-while loop. This indicates the end of the loop code; in a while loop, the loop code doesn't end until the last statement inside the curly brackets.

In the next chapter, we'll look at some more complex examples of looping and flow control.

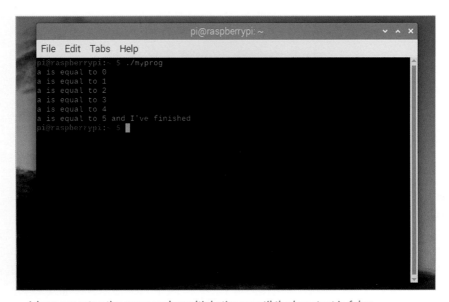

▲ A loop executes the same code multiple times until the loop test is false

Chapter 4

More advanced flow control

For loops and case statements – more advanced
ways of controlling the flow of a program

The if statement and while loop described in the previous chapter are fairly simple control structures. In this chapter, we're going to look at a few more complex structures that can help to make your code shorter and reduce the amount of typing you need to do...

Although the while loop we saw in the previous article is very useful, the *for* loop tends to be favoured by many programmers, as it puts all the logic controlling the loop in one place. Here's an example:

```c
#include <stdio.h>

void main (void)
{
  int a;

  for (a = 0; a < 5; a++)
  {
    printf ("a is equal to %d\n", a);
  }
  printf ("a is equal to %d and I've finished\n", a);
}
```

This isn't all that different from a while loop, but all of the control for the loop lives in the round brackets after the **for** keyword. This contains three statements, separated by semicolons: in order, these are the *initial condition*, the *test*, and the *increment*.

a = 0 is the initial condition; the variable **a** is initialised to 0 at the start of the loop.

a < 5 is the test, just like in a while loop. This is checked on each iteration of the loop, and the loop code is only executed if the test evaluates to true; as soon as the test is false, execution continues after the curly bracket at the end of the loop code.

a++ is the increment; this is code which is executed at the end of each iteration of the loop, before the test is evaluated again. In this case, it adds 1 to **a**.

So when this for loop runs, what happens? First, **a** is set to 0. The test is then checked: is **a** (which is 0) less than 5? Yes it is, so the code inside the curly brackets is executed, and the value of **a** is printed. Finally, the increment is applied, meaning 1 is added to **a**.

The test is then repeated. If true, the loop code is executed again, and the increment is again applied; this repeats over and over until the test is false, at which point execution continues after the closing curly bracket.

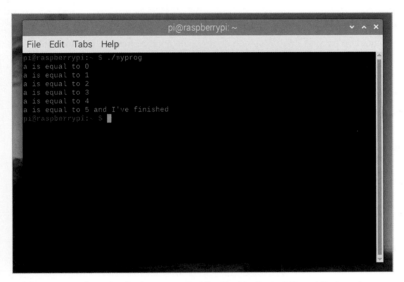

▲ The output when the for loop runs is identical to that of the while loop in the previous chapter – they both do exactly the same thing

In terms of what they do, for loops and while loops are pretty much identical; both wrap up a section of code you want to run more than once in some logic that controls how many times it runs. You can use whichever makes the most sense, or whichever looks tidiest to you!

MULTIPLE INITIALISATIONS

You can initialise multiple variables in a for loop – just separate them by commas. So if you want to set two variables at the start of the loop, you can use:

```
for (a = 0, b = 1; <test>; <increment>)
```

Switch statements

One thing that you quite often want to do is to test a variable against several values, and do different things based on each of them. You can do this with a set of nested if statements:

```c
#include <stdio.h>

void main (void)
{
  unsigned int a = 0;

  if (a == 0)
  {
    printf ("a is equal to 0\n");
  }
  else if (a == 1)
  {
    printf ("a is equal to 1\n");
  }
  else
  {
    printf ("a is greater than 1\n");
  }
}
```

That does start to get pretty long-winded, though, so C provides a neater way of doing this, called a *switch* statement.

```c
#include <stdio.h>

void main (void)
{
  unsigned int a = 0;
```

```
switch (a)
{
  case 0 :    printf ("a is equal to 0\n");
              break;
  case 1 :    printf ("a is equal to 1\n");
              break;
  default :   printf ("a is greater than 1\n");
}
}
```

This does exactly the same as the example above with multiple if statements, but is a lot shorter. So how does it work?

The opening line consists of the keyword **switch**, with the name of a variable in round brackets. This is the variable which will be tested against the various cases.

The body of the switch statement is a number of **case** statements. The variable **a** is compared against each case in turn; if it matches the value immediately after the word **case**, then the lines of code after the colon are executed.

The final case is just called **default** – every switch statement should include a default case as the final one in the list, and this is the code which is executed if none of the other cases matches.

Notice that the last line in each case section is the word **break** – this is very important. The keyword **break** tells the compiler that you want to 'break out' of the switch statement at this point; that is, to stop executing code inside the switch and to resume execution after the closing curly bracket. If you forget to include the break statements, every case after the one you wanted will execute, as well as the one you wanted. Try it by compiling the code above and running it – you'll see the following in the terminal:

```
a is equal to 0
```

Now remove the two break statements, so the switch looks like:

```
switch (a)
{
  case 0 :    printf ("a is equal to 0\n");
  case 1 :    printf ("a is equal to 1\n");
  default :   printf ("a is greater than 1\n");
}
```

...and run it again – you'll now see:

```
a is equal to 0
a is equal to 1
a is greater than 1
```

Not what you expected! This is another common bug in C code – forgetting the break statements in your cases can result in very unexpected behaviour. But this can also be useful; programmers will sometimes structure a switch statement with code that they want to execute in multiple different cases, and deliberately leave out the break statements.

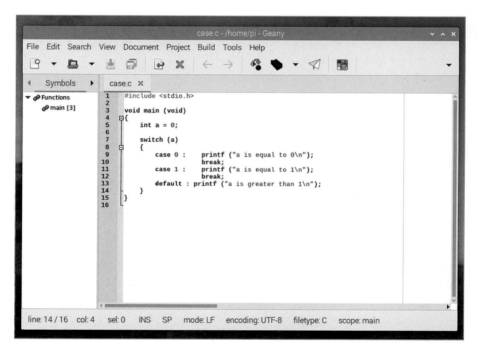

▲ Don't forget the break statements at the end of each case in your switch statements!

YOUR FAVOURITE LOOP...

All three types of loop in C – while, do-while, and for – can be used in pretty much any situation where a loop is needed; choose whichever you like. Some people prefer to use one type of loop for everything; others pick and choose whichever looks tidiest for each circumstance. There are no wrong choices!

Leaving a loop early

The break statement has one other use: it can be used inside while and for loops to break out of them. Look at this example:

```c
#include <stdio.h>

void main (void)
{
  int a = 0;

  while (1)
  {
    printf ("a is equal to %d\n", a);
    a++;
    if (a == 5)
    {
      break;
    }
  }
  printf ("a is equal to %d and I've finished\n", a);
}
```

So we have a while loop in which the test is just the value 1; this is a non-zero value, and so is always true. If you enclose code inside curly brackets after a **while (1)** statement, the loop will never end; it will keep running forever. But in this case we have provided an alternative way to end the loop; we test the value of **a** inside the loop itself in an if statement, and if **a** is equal to 5, we call **break**. This causes the loop to end and execution to continue with the statement after the loop. A break statement like this can be useful to leave a loop early in the event of an error, for example.

CONTINUE

The keyword **continue** can be used in a loop instead of break, but instead of breaking out of the loop, it skips all the rest of the code in the current iteration, and returns to the test case at the start of the loop. Among other things, this can be useful to speed up your code.

Chapter 5
Pointers

Pointers – variables have addresses as well as names...

The term *pointer* has struck fear into the heart of many a beginner C programmer, but once you've got your head around them, pointers are a very useful feature of the language. They aren't actually that complicated in reality, but it's easy to get confused when using them, so let's try to avoid that...

Remember when we looked at the declaration of variables? Declaring a variable – telling the compiler what type it is and what it's called – before you can use it is necessary in C, because the declaration enables the compiler to allocate a block of memory to store the variable. So for every variable you declare, there's a block of memory which is set aside by the compiler for that variable, and the compiler remembers which particular block of memory is used for each variable.

What is a pointer?

A pointer is just the address of a block of memory with a variable in it; that's all there is to it. So if you declare a variable and a pointer to that variable, you can access the value in that block of memory in two ways: either with the variable name, or with the pointer.

Let's look at a simple example:

```
#include <stdio.h>

void main (void)
{
  int a;
  int *ptr_to_a;

  ptr_to_a = &a;

  a = 5;
  printf ("The value of a is %d\n", a);

  *ptr_to_a = 6;
  printf ("The value of a is %d\n", a);
```

```
    printf ("The value of ptr_to_a is %d\n", ptr_to_a);
    printf ("It stores the value %d\n", *ptr_to_a);
    printf ("The address of a is %d\n", &a);
}
```

Taking it line by line, the first line is one we're already familiar with: we declare an integer variable called **a**. But what's this?

```
int *ptr_to_a;
```

This looks like it's declaring another integer variable, doesn't it? But look more carefully; the asterisk (*****) at the start of the variable name indicates that this is not declaring an integer variable, but a pointer to an integer variable.

So we now have an integer variable called **a**, and we have a pointer to an integer variable, called **ptr_to_a**. But neither of these actually has a value in it yet: they are both uninitialised. It's all very well calling the pointer **ptr_to_a**, but it has no idea what (or where) **a** is, so we'll fix that with the next line.

```
ptr_to_a = &a;
```

This is the important bit! In C, the symbol **&** before a variable name means *address of the variable*, so **&a** means 'the address in memory of the variable **a**'. And as we said above, a pointer is the address of a variable. So this line initialises **ptr_to_a** to be the address of **a**; **ptr_to_a** is now a valid pointer to the variable **a**, so we can now use it.

The next two lines are familiar: we set **a** to be 5, and just to check that worked, we print its value. So let's try doing the same thing, but with the pointer.

```
*ptr_to_a = 6;
```

That asterisk again, but used in a slightly different way from before. When declaring a variable, putting an asterisk before its name indicates that the variable is a pointer. But once the pointer exists, putting an asterisk in front of its name means *the variable pointed to by this pointer*; this is known as *dereferencing* the pointer. So this line tells the compiler to set the variable pointed to by the pointer **ptr_to_a** to 6. We know that the variable pointed to by **ptr_to_a** is **a**; we set that up a couple of lines back, and so this line is just another way of setting **a** to 6; indeed, if we print the value of **a**, we find it has changed to 6.

The next lines will hopefully help you get the relationship between pointers, variables, and addresses clear in your mind.

```
printf ("The value of ptr_to_a is %d\n", ptr_to_a);
```

In this line, we're printing the value of **ptr_to_a**; not the value it's pointing at, but the value of the pointer itself. This prints a very large number, as it's the address in memory where **a** can be found.

```
printf ("It stores the value %d\n", *ptr_to_a);
```

In this line, we're printing the value pointed to by **ptr_to_a**; note the asterisk before the name. This prints the value of **a**.

```
printf ("The address of a is %d\n", &a);
```

Finally, in this line we're printing the address of **a** itself; note the **&** sign before the name. Again, this prints a very large number, the same as the value of **ptr_to_a** we printed above.

* AND &

When I was first learning about pointers, I found it helpful to say out loud what a line of code was doing – an * is 'what is pointed to by', and an & is 'the address of'. Once you've got those two ideas fixed in your head, you've pretty much understood pointers!

The crucial thing to remember when working with pointers is this: you can't just declare a pointer, as you need to also declare and associate the variable you want it to point to. When a pointer is created, it points at a random location in memory; if you try to write something to it, you can cause all sorts of errors up to and including crashing the computer completely! Always make sure your pointers are pointing at something before doing anything with them.

MEMORY

Pointers are one of the ways C allows (or in some cases forces) you to think about what the actual hardware of your computer is doing – a good understanding of pointers gives you a good understanding of how the compiler handles memory.

```
pi@raspberrypi: ~                                    v  ^  x
File  Edit  Tabs  Help
pi@raspberrypi:~ $ gcc -o myprog point.c
pi@raspberrypi:~ $ ./myprog
The value of a is 5
The value of a is 6
The value of ptr_to_a is 3200045560
It stores the value 6
The address of a is 3200045560
pi@raspberrypi:~ $
```

▲ The example code shows clearly the relationship between a pointer and the actual address
in memory of a variable – note that the address of **a** is identical to the value of the pointer.
(The actual address will probably be different when you run the code, but the pointer and
the address will still have the same value.)

ALWAYS HAVE SOMETHING TO POINT TO!

It's worth stressing this again: a pointer is not a piece of memory, it's just an address of
memory. If you want to do anything with a pointer, you need to declare something for it to
point to as well as the pointer itself.

Void pointers and casting

You can also define a pointer without saying what type of variable it's pointing to; this is a
void pointer, written as **void** *. If you think about it, this makes sense: a pointer is just an
address in memory, so we don't necessarily need to know what is at that memory. To use a
void pointer, you need to *cast* it. *Casting* is telling the compiler how to interpret what is at the
memory location pointed to by a pointer – you tell the compiler what sort of variable it should
expect to find there. Here's an example:

```
#include <stdio.h>

void main (void)
{
```

```
int intval = 255958283;
void *vptr = &intval;

printf ("The value at vptr as an int is %d\n", *((int *) vptr));
printf ("The value at vptr as a char is %d\n", *((char *) vptr));
}
```

We initialise the void pointer **vptr** to point to an integer variable called **intval**.

In the first **printf** statement, we insert **(int *)** in front of **vptr** before we dereference it using *****. This casts **vptr** to an integer pointer, and so the value of **intval** is printed as an integer.

In the second **printf** statement, we insert **(char *)** in front of **vptr** before we dereference it. This casts **vptr** to a char pointer, and so what's printed is the value of the char which makes up the first byte of **intval**.

What do you use pointers for?

That's really all there is to pointers, other than to ask why bother? We can already access a variable with its name, so why do we need to have some complicated alternative way of getting to the contents of a variable?

There are several ways in which pointers are useful, which we will explore in more detail in later chapters. But a few of the important ones are:

> **function calls** – in the next chapter we will look at how to split up C code into functions; pointers are very useful for allowing a function to return multiple values.
> **string handling** – in C, a string is a continuous block of memory with a letter stored in each byte; pointers make it possible to perform efficient operations on strings.
> **arrays** – in C, an array variable can be used to store a list of values of the same type, which like a string is stored in a continuous block of memory; pointers make accessing arrays easier and more efficient.

INCREMENTING POINTERS

You can use **++** and **--** on pointers, but you need to be careful. **(*a)++** increments the value pointed to by **a**, but ***(a++)** increments the pointer itself rather than the value it points at – this will move **a** to point at the memory address immediately after **a**.

Chapter 6
Functions

Functions – how to split your code up into easy bite-sized chunks...

Up until now, all the examples we've looked at have had one single function, **main**, with all the code in it. This is perfectly valid for small, simple programs, but it's not really practical once you get more than a few tens of lines, and it's a waste of space if you need to do the same thing more than once. Splitting code up into separate functions makes it more readable and enables easy reuse.

We've already seen functions used; the **main** function is a standard C function, albeit with a special name. We've also seen the **printf** function called by our examples. So how do we create and use a function of our own? Here's an example:

```c
#include <stdio.h>

int sum (int a, int b)
{
  int res;
  res = a + b;
  return res;
}

void main (void)
{
  int y = 2;
  int z = sum (5, y);

  printf ("The sum of 5 and %d is %d\n", y, z);
}
```

This includes both the **main** function and a second function called **sum**. In both cases, the structure of the function is the same: a line defining the value returned by the function, the function name, and the function arguments, followed by a block of code enclosed within curly brackets, which is what the function actually does.

What's in a function?

Let's look at the **sum** function:

```
int sum (int a, int b)
```

The definition of a function has three parts. The first part is the type of the value returned by the function: in this case, an `int`. The second part is the name of the function: in this case, **sum**. Finally, within round brackets are the arguments to the function, separated by commas, and each given with its type: in this case, two integer arguments, **a** and **b**.

The rest of the function is between the curly brackets.

```
int res;
```

This declares a *local variable* for the function, an integer called **res**. This is a variable which can only be used locally, within the function itself. Variables declared within a function definition can only be used within that function; if you try to read or write **res** within the **main** function, you'll get an error. (You could declare another `int` called **res** within the **main** function, but this would be a different variable called **res** from the one within the **sum** function, and would get very confusing, so it's not recommended!)

```
res = a + b;
```

This should be obvious! Note that **a** and **b** are the two defined arguments of the function. When a function is called, a local copy of the arguments is made and used within the function. If you change the values of **a** or **b** within the function (which is a perfectly valid thing to do), that only affects the value of **a** and **b** within this function; it doesn't change the values that the arguments had in the function from which it was called.

```
return res;
```

Finally, we need to return the result. The function was defined to return an integer, so it must call the **return** statement with an integer value to be returned to the calling function. A function doesn't have to return a value; if the return type is set to **void**, it returns nothing.

There's no need for a **return** statement in a function with a **void** return type: the function will return when it reaches the last line; however, if you want to return early (in the event of an error, for example), you just call **return** with no value after it.

VARIABLE SCOPE

If you declare a variable within a function, it's only usable within that function, not within any functions which call the function, or within functions called by the function. This is known as the *scope* of a variable: the parts of the code in which it's valid.

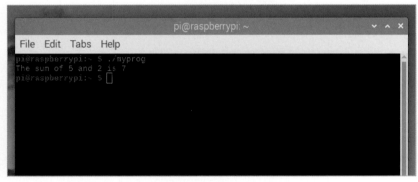

▲ The **main** function prints out the values returned by the **sum** function

Calling a function

Let's look at how we call the function from **main**:

```
int z = sum (5, y);
```

The **sum** function returns an integer, so we set an integer variable equal to it. The arguments we supply to the function are inside round brackets, and in the same order as in the function definition; so in this case, **a** is 5, and **b** is the value of **y**.

Can you return more than one result from a function? You can only return one value, but you can also use pointers to pass multiple items of data back to the calling function. Consider this example:

```
#include <stdio.h>

int sum_and_diff (int a, int b, int *res)
{
  int sum;
  sum = a + b;
```

```
  *res = a - b;
  return sum;
}

void main (void)
{
  int b = 2;
  int diff;

  printf ("The sum of 5 and %d is %d\n", b,
      sum_and_diff (5, b, &diff));
  printf ("The difference of 5 and %d is %d\n", b, diff);
}
```

We've modified the **sum** function to calculate both the sum and the difference of the arguments. The sum is returned as before, but we're also passing the difference back using a pointer. Remember that the arguments to a function are local variables; even if you change one in the function, it has no effect on the value passed by the calling function. This is why pointers are useful: by passing a pointer, the function doesn't change the value of the pointer itself, but it can change the value in the variable to which it's pointing.

So we call the function with the same two arguments as before, but we add a third one, a pointer to the variable where we want to write the difference calculated by the function. In the function, we have this line:

```
*res = a - b;
```

The difference is written to the variable to which **res** is a pointer.

In the **main** function, we call the **sum_and_diff** function like this:

```
sum_and_diff (5, b, &diff)
```

We provide the address of the integer **diff** as the pointer argument to the **sum_and_diff** function; when the difference is calculated, it's written into the variable **diff** in the **main** function.

RETURNING VALUES

A function can return a single value, or no value at all. If you define the function as returning **void**, there's no need to use a **return** statement in it, but you'll get an error if you don't include a **return** of the correct type in a non-void function.

▲ By using a pointer as one argument, the `sum_and_diff` function can return both the sum and difference of the arguments

MODIFYING ARGUMENTS

Arguments are local variables within a function. If you want a function to modify the arguments you give it, make each argument you want to modify a pointer to a variable; you can then read the value pointed to within the function, and write the changed value back to the same pointer.

Order matters

One thing to bear in mind when defining functions is that the compiler reads files from top to bottom, and you need to tell it about a function before you can use it. In the examples above, this is automatic, as the definition of the **sum** and **sum_and_diff** functions is before the first call to them in **main**.

But in larger files, when multiple functions call multiple other functions, this gets complicated; it's not always easy to make sure the function definitions are all in the right order. To avoid this, C allows you to *declare* functions before they are used.

A function declaration is just the definition of the function, minus the function code within the curly brackets. So for the **sum_and_diff** function, the declaration would be:

```
int sum_and_diff (int a, int b, int *res);
```

Note the semicolon at the end! Function declarations are included at the top of the file; when the compiler finds a function declaration, it knows that at some point a function with this name, arguments, and return type will be defined, so it then knows how to handle a call to it, even if it hasn't yet seen the definition itself.

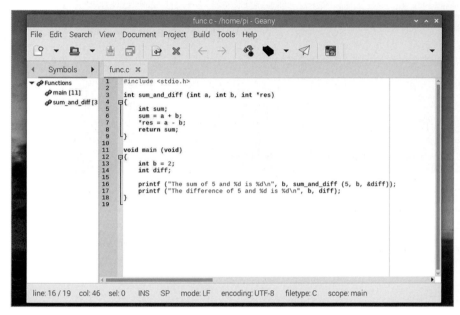

▲ You can use a function call wherever a variable of the same type as the value returned by the function could be used – in the code here, a call to `sum_and_diff` replaces an integer value in the arguments to `printf`

Chapter 7

Arrays and strings

How to handle arrays (lists of values) and strings
(lists of letters) in C

The variables we have looked at so far are all single numeric values. In this chapter,
we're going to look at how C handles lists of values, and that leads into using lists of
letters to store and manipulate text strings.

An *array* is a single variable which stores multiple different values of the same type;
the individual values are accessed by *indexing* the array. An array can have one or more
dimensions; a one-dimensional array is a single list of values, while a two-dimensional array is
a list of lists of values, and so on.

An array is declared in C by putting the size of each dimension in square brackets after the
variable name. So,

```
int a[10];
```

...is a list of ten integers, while

```
int b[5][6];
```

...is a list of five lists, each of which contains six integers.

When accessing the elements inside an array, the array index – the number inside the
bracket – starts at 0. So the ten integers contained within array **a** above are referred to as
a[0], **a[1]**, **a[2]**, and so on up to **a[9]**. The compiler will quite happily allow you to read or
write **a[10]**, **a[11]**, or indeed **a[**any number you like**]**, but these are all outside the memory
which was allocated when the array was declared, so writing to them is a really bad idea!

Arrays and pointers

This brings us on to the relationship between pointers and arrays. The name of an array is
effectively a pointer to the first element of the array. Remember that a pointer is the address
of a variable in memory? Well, an array is a contiguous block of memory which contains all the
elements of the array in order, so you can use a pointer to access it. (In fact, even if you use
values in square brackets to access it, the compiler treats those as a pointer anyway.) Here's
an example:

```
#include <stdio.h>

void main (void)
{
    int a[10];
    int count;

    for (count = 0; count < 10; count++)
    {
        a[count] = count * 10 + count;
    }

    printf ("The first and second elements of a are %d and %d\n",
        a[0], a[1]);
    printf ("Or, as pointers, %d and %d\n", *a, *(a+1));
}
```

This fills the ten values of **a** with the numbers 0, 11, 22, 33, and so on, and then reads **a[0]** and **a[1]**. It then reads the same values using **a** as a pointer, and you can see if you run the code that they are identical.

With a two- (or more) dimensional array, you need to consider how the compiler arranges the dimensions in memory; it does so by grouping the elements at the rightmost index of the array together. With the array **b[5][6]**, **b** itself points at **b[0][0]**. **b+1** points at **b[0][1]**; **b+5** points at **b[0][5]**; and **b+6** points at **b[1][0]**.

▲ Array elements are stored sequentially in memory, with the array name a pointer to the first element. Multidimensional array elements are stored with the elements with neighbouring values in the rightmost index next to each other

You can initialise an array at the same time as you declare it by putting the values in curly brackets, so:

```
int a[10] = { 0, 11, 22, 33, 44, 55, 66, 77, 88, 99 };
```

But note that this only works when the array is first declared; once it exists, you can't use this shortcut and will need to iterate through the array indices, setting each value in turn.

KEEP INSIDE YOUR ARRAY

One of the nastiest sources of crashes and bugs in C is creating an array and then writing past the end of it. The compiler won't stop you writing to memory off the end of an array, and doing so can have serious consequences. Always make sure your array indices fit inside your array.

NAMES ARE POINTERS

Remember that the name of an array or a string is just a pointer to the first element of the array or string in question, and can be used in the same way as any other pointer; it can be incremented and decremented, or dereferenced to find the value to which it points.

Strings

In C, a string is just another array; it's an array of single characters. As we saw in chapter 2, a character is a specific type in C, called **char**; this holds a single byte, which is enough to hold an alphanumeric character. So a string with ten characters would be:

```
char mystring[10];
```

Or, to initialise it at the same time:

```
char mystring[10] = "thestring";
```

One important thing to remember is that a string in C must always end with a byte set to zero, and that the memory required to hold this final zero (called the *string terminator*) must be allocated when you declare the string. So **mystring**, which is declared as an array of ten chars, can only actually hold text of nine or fewer letters.

mystring

't'	'h'	'e'	's'	't'	'r'	'i'	'n'	'g'	0

▲ Strings are stored as an array of single characters, with the element after the last character set to zero

You can use the index in square brackets to access individual characters in a string, or you can use a pointer. Here's an example of using pointers to join two strings together:

```c
#include <stdio.h>

void main (void)
{
  char str1[10] = "first";
  char str2[10] = "second";
  char str3[20];

  char *src, *dst;

  src = str1;
  dst = str3;
  while (*src != 0)
  {
    *dst = *src;
    src++;
    dst++;
  }
  src = str2;
  while (*src != 0)
  {
    *dst = *src;
    src++;
    dst++;
  }
  *dst = 0;

  printf ("%s + %s = %s\n", str1, str2, str3);
}
```

First, we create two strings – **str1** is 'first' and **str2** is 'second' – and we allocate an empty string, **str3**, to put the result in.

We then create a pair of **char** pointers, and point **src** at the start of **str1** (the 'f' of 'first') and **dst** at the start of the empty **str3**. We then loop, copying what's at **src** to **dst**, and then moving both pointers forward by one, until we find the zero that terminates **str1**.

We then point **src** at **str2**, and do the same thing again, until we find the zero at the end of **str2**. Finally, we write a zero to the end of **str3** to terminate it. Note the new format specifier used to print strings; **%s** is used to print a string, and will display every character from the pointer supplied as an argument, up to the first terminating zero it finds. (If you want to print a single character, you can use the format specifier **%c**.)

Writing to strings

Because the name of a string variable is only a pointer to the first character of the string, you can't just use an equals sign to set the value of a complete string. You can initialise a string variable at the time you declare it, as above, but what if you want to set or change it later?

There are a few ways to do this, but the most useful is the **sprintf** function; this is a version of the **printf** function we have already seen, which writes arbitrary text to string variables. The only difference is that the first argument it takes is the name of a string variable, and it writes to that instead of to the terminal:

```
#include <stdio.h>

void main (void)
{
  int val = 12;
  char string[50];

  sprintf (string, "The value of val is %d\n", val);
  printf ("%s", string);
}
```

The **sprintf** function will automatically add the terminating zero at the end of any string you create with it.

TERMINATING STRINGS

Always remember that the memory you allocate for a string needs to be long enough to hold all the characters, plus one extra to store the terminating zero. If you're manipulating strings yourself with pointers, make sure you remember to write the zero at the end of any string you create.

In the next chapter, we'll look at some of the functions provided in C's string handling library to make working with strings easier.

Chapter 8

The string library

Using the C string library to simplify common operations on strings

I n the previous chapter, we saw how to access strings using pointers. This works perfectly well, and gives you a good understanding of how pointers work, but it's a bit long-winded. Fortunately, C provides a library of useful string functions, which save a lot of typing!

In the last chapter, we saw how to join two strings together using pointers. We're going to do the same thing using the string handling library. Here's the code rewritten using string library functions:

```c
#include <stdio.h>
#include <string.h>

void main (void)
{
  char str1[10] = "first";
  char str2[10] = "second";
  char str3[20];

  strcpy (str3, str1);
  strcat (str3, str2);

  printf ("%s + %s = %s\n", str1, str2, str3);
}
```

KEEP INSIDE YOUR STRING

The string library functions won't generally prevent you from writing off the end of a string; just as when using pointers, when using library functions you still need to make sure your string variables are large enough for the values you're writing into them.

That's a lot shorter! Note the **#include <string.h>** at the start, which tells the compiler we want to use functions from the string library.

This shows us two string functions. **strcpy** ('string copy') copies the string at the second argument to the start of string at the first argument. **strcat** ('string concatenate') does the same thing, but instead of copying to the start of the first argument, it finds the terminating zero of the first argument and starts copying to its location, thus joining the two strings together.

DON'T OVERWRITE

It looks like it ought to be possible to use **strcpy** and **strcat** to copy part of a string over itself – **strcpy (a + 1, a)**, for example. Don't try it! The source and destination buffers for **strcpy** and **strcat** must be completely separate areas of memory; if not, their behaviour is unpredictable.

Comparing strings

Another common requirement is to be able to compare two strings to see if they are the same. As we've already seen, we can compare numeric values with the == operator, but this doesn't work with strings. Remember that the name of a string is really just a pointer to a location in memory containing the string, so using == to compare two strings will only tell you if they're at the same place in memory, not if two strings at different locations are the same.

You can use == to compare two **char** variables, and a string is an array of chars, so it's possible to write a simple piece of code that compares each character in a string in turn:

```
#include <stdio.h>

void main (void)
{
  char str1[10] = "first";
  char str2[10] = "fire";
  char *ptr1 = str1, *ptr2 = str2;

  while (*ptr1 != 0 && *ptr2 != 0)
  {
    if (*ptr1 != *ptr2)
    {
      break;
    }
    ptr1++;
```

```
      ptr2++;
   }

   if (*ptr1 == 0 && *ptr2 == 0)
   {
      printf ("The two strings are identical.\n");
   }
   else
   {
      printf ("The two strings are different.\n");
   }
}
```

But that's a bit tedious to write out every time, so the string library can do this for you with the function **strcmp** (for 'string compare'). Here's how you use it:

```
#include <stdio.h>
#include <string.h>

void main (void)
{
   char str1[10] = "first";
   char str2[10] = "fire";
   if (strcmp (str1, str2) == 0)
   {
      printf ("The two strings are identical.\n");
   }
   else
   {
      printf ("The two strings are different.\n");
   }
}
```

strcmp takes two strings as arguments, and returns a 0 if they're the same; it returns a non-zero value if not.

What about if you just want to compare the first few characters of a string, not the whole string? There's a library function for that, too: **strncmp** (for 'string numbered compare').

This works in exactly the same way as **strcmp**, but it takes a third argument, an integer giving the number of characters to compare. So **strncmp ("first", "fire", 4)** would return a non-zero value, while **strncmp ("first", "fire", 3)** would return a 0.

> ## IGNORING CASE
>
> There are versions of **strcmp** and **strncmp** which ignore the case of the letters in the strings being compared; they're called **strcasecmp** and **strncasecmp**, respectively. They take the same arguments and return the same values.

Reading values from a string

We saw in the previous chapter that we can use **sprintf** to write variables into a string; what about being able to read variables back out of a string? The function **sscanf** ('string scan formatted') does that for you. Here's how it works:

```
#include <stdio.h>

void main (void)
{
  int val;
  char string[10] = "250";

  sscanf (string, "%d", &val);
  printf ("The value in the string is %d\n", val);
}
```

sscanf uses exactly the same format specifiers as **printf**. One important difference, though, is that the arguments to **sscanf** must all be pointers to variables, rather than variables themselves. As always, a function can never change the values of variables provided as arguments, but it can write to their destinations if they are pointers.

▼ The **sscanf** library function is used here with the %d format specifier to read the decimal value 250 out of a string

You can check whether **sscanf** was able to match the format specifiers with the string provided by looking at the value it returns; **sscanf** returns the number of values it successfully read. So for example, if a format specifier of **%d** is provided but the string supplied doesn't start with a decimal number, **sscanf** will write nothing to the supplied pointer and will return 0; if the string supplied does start with a decimal number, **sscanf** will return 1.

The format string supplied to **sscanf** can contain multiple format specifiers and even other text:

```c
#include <stdio.h>

void main (void)
{
  int val;
  char result[10];
  char string[25] = "The first number is 1";

  if (sscanf (string, "The %s number is %d", result, &val) == 2)
  {
    printf ("String : %s Value : %d\n", result, val);
  }
  else
  {
    printf ("I couldn't find two values in that string.\n");
  }
}
```

Note that, slightly inconsistently, the **%s** format specifier denotes a pointer to a string in both **printf** and **sscanf**, while the **%d** specifier denotes a variable in **printf** but a pointer in **sscanf**.

One thing to note about **sscanf** is that it's in the standard I/O library, not the string handling library, so you don't need **#include <string.h>** to use it.

SSCANF STRINGS

The **%s** format specifier matches a set of non-whitespace characters in **sscanf**; it will extract the first set of letters, numbers, or punctuation up to the first space, tab, or newline it finds in the string being scanned. A space in the format string matches one or more whitespace characters, not just a single space.

▾ `sscanf` reads numeric values and words out of a formatted string, allowing you to parse text from elsewhere. Remember that all the arguments to `sscanf` must be pointers

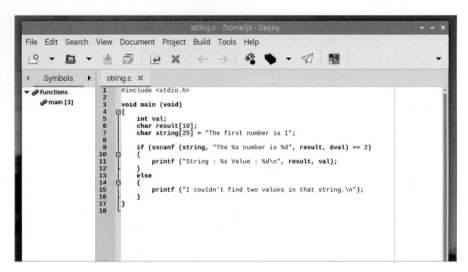

How long is a (piece of) string?

One final useful string handling function is **strlen** (for 'string length'); as the name suggests, this tells you how many characters there are in a string, excluding the terminating zero character.

```
#include <stdio.h>
#include <string.h>

void main (void)
{
  char str1[10] = "first";

  printf ("The length of the string '%s' is %d\n", str1,
      strlen (str1));
}
```

All the operations we've looked at here are possible by manually manipulating pointers; the string library just makes them easier and will make your code shorter. If you find yourself moving pointers around strings in a program, always check the string library to make sure you're not reinventing the wheel!

Chapter 9
User input

Reading and interpreting input from the user

We've seen the **printf** function used a lot in previous chapters; it's the standard way of writing formatted text output from a program to the console, the command line from which you run the program. But what if you want to get input from the user? How do we read what the user types into the console?

In the last chapter, we looked at the **sscanf** function which reads values from a string. There's an equivalent function called **scanf**, which reads values directly from the console, as in the following example:

```c
#include <stdio.h>

void main (void)
{
  char input[256];
  int age;

  printf ("What is your name, user?\n");
  scanf ("%s", input);

  printf ("Hello, %s. How old are you?\n", input);
  scanf ("%d", &age);

  printf ("Well, %s, you look young for %d...\n", input, age);
}
```

scanf works exactly like **sscanf**, but has one fewer argument, as it reads from the console rather than from a string.

However, it's not really the best way of getting console input; it only really works if you have a user who types in exactly what you expect. Unfortunately, users have a nasty tendency to type in things you aren't expecting, and **scanf** doesn't cope well with this. For example, in the code above, if the user types in 257 characters when asked for their name, they will overflow the space allocated for the input string, and bad things may happen...

STDIN AND STDOUT

We talk about `stdin` in this chapter, which is the 'standard input' stream: what the user types at the console. You may sometimes see references to `stdout`, which is the 'standard output' stream – as you might expect, this is output which is printed to the console, usually via `printf`.

A better way

A better approach is to read each line the user enters into a buffer string, and then use `sscanf` to read values from that string. The C library function `fgets` is useful for this. Have a look at this example:

```c
#include <stdio.h>

void main (void)
{
  char input[256], name[256];
  int age;

  printf ("What is your name, user?\n");
  fgets (input, 256, stdin);
  sscanf (input, "%s", name);

  printf ("Hello, %s. How old are you?\n", name);
  while (1)
  {
    fgets (input, 256, stdin);
    if (sscanf (input, "%d", &age) == 1) break;
    printf ("I don't recognise that as an age - try again!\n");
  }

  printf ("Well, %s, you look young for %d...\n", name, age);
}
```

`fgets` takes three arguments. The first is the buffer into which it should store the input. The second is the maximum number of bytes it will write into that buffer; this is useful to prevent the overflow situation mentioned above. Finally, it takes an argument telling it where to read from; in this case, this is set to `stdin` (short for 'standard input'), which tells it to read from the console.

So each time we ask the user for input, we use **fgets** to read up to 256 characters of whatever they type (up to the point at which they press the **ENTER** key), and we then use **sscanf** to interpret it. Additionally, when asking for the user's age, we use the value returned by **sscanf** (described in the previous chapter) to check that the user has entered what you expect, and loop until they give a valid answer. You can use this method to interpret pretty much anything a user types, and to safely handle all the cases where they type something unexpected!

SCANF

Just like **sscanf**, **scanf** returns an integer indicating how many values it successfully read, which you can use to check for errors. One problem is that **scanf** only removes matched values from the input buffer, so if a **scanf** fails to match anything, what the user typed will be read again on the next call to **scanf**. It really is easier to use **fgets** and **sscanf**!

Reading parameters

There's another way to get input to your program, which is to supply it as a parameter when you start the program from the command line.

At this point, I have to admit to not having been entirely honest for the last eight chapters... I've always shown the definition of the **main** function as:

```
void main (void)
```

This works, as you've seen, but it isn't strictly correct. The strict definition of **main** looks like this:

```
int main (int argc, char *argv[])
```

But let's be honest: if I'd shown you that in chapter 1, you'd have run a mile, wouldn't you? So what does it all mean?

First off, we can see that **main** returns an integer; this is a success or failure code which some operating systems can use for processing in a shell script or the like. Traditionally, if a program succeeds, **main** returns 0, and if it fails, it returns a non-zero error code. For programs that run on their own, you really don't need to worry about it!

What's more useful are the other two arguments. **argc** is an integer, and this is the number of parameters which were provided on the command line when the program was started. Strangely, the number includes the program name itself, so this value is always 1 or more; if parameters were provided, it will be 2 or more.

`char *argv[];` now that's confusing, right? This is actually a composite of a few things we've already seen. There's a * in there, so it's a pointer; the type is **char**, so there are characters in it, and there are square brackets, so it's an array...

This is actually an array of pointers to characters; each element of the array is a string, and each string is one of the parameters provided to the program.

It's probably easier to understand that in practice:

```c
#include <stdio.h>

int main (int argc, char *argv[])
{
  int param = 0;
  while (param < argc)
  {
    printf ("Parameter %d is %s\n", param, argv[param]);
    param++;
  }
  return 0;
}
```

Try running this as before, just by typing its name. Then try typing other things after the name on the command line and see what the program prints.

Here's an example of a (very) simple calculator written using program parameters:

```c
#include <stdio.h>

int main (int argc, char *argv[])
{
  int arg1, arg2;
  if (argc == 4)
  {
    sscanf (argv[1], "%d", &arg1);
    sscanf (argv[3], "%d", &arg2);
    if (*argv[2] == '+') printf ("%d\n", arg1 + arg2);
    if (*argv[2] == '-') printf ("%d\n", arg1 - arg2);
    if (*argv[2] == 'x') printf ("%d\n", arg1 * arg2);
    if (*argv[2] == '/') printf ("%d\n", arg1 / arg2);
  }
  return 0;
}
```

Note that we use ***argv[2]** to get the first character of the second parameter. This should only ever be a single character, but because each of the arguments can be a string, **argv[2]** (without the asterisk) is a pointer to a character, not the single character required for a comparison using ==.

Make sure you separate the arguments from the operator with spaces so they're identified as separate parameters: **<progname> 2 + 2** rather than **<progname> 2+2**.

GET THE NUMBER RIGHT

Remember that the first item in the **argv** array – **argv[0]** – is the name of the program itself, not the first parameter. The actual parameters start at **argv[1]**.

▲ The **argc** and **argv** arguments to the **main** function can be used to access parameters typed on the command line when the program is run

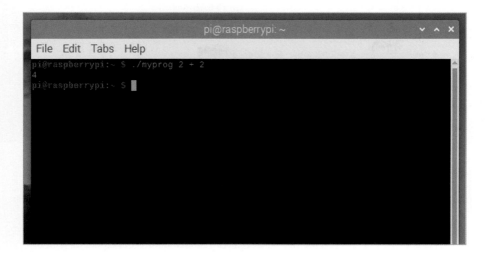

pi@raspberrypi: ~

File Edit Tabs Help

```
pi@raspberrypi:~ $ ./myprog 2 + 2
4
pi@raspberrypi:~ $
```

▲ The calculator reads the two values and the operator from the `argv` array and prints the result

CHECKING RETURN VALUES

In Linux, the return value from a program isn't shown, but is stored and can be read from the command line. If you type `echo $?` immediately after running a program, the value the program returned will be shown. Return values are mainly useful if you're calling programs from scripts.

Chapter 10
File input and output
Reading from and writing to files

In the previous chapter, we looked at how to get input from the user at the console. In this chapter, we'll look at the other common method of input and output in C: reading and writing files.

Many programs need to be able to access files on the host computer's disk; even if it's just for saving user preferences and the like, file access is a fundamental requirement for a lot of programming tasks.

In C, files are accessed by use of *file pointers*. A file pointer contains all the information required to access a file: both its name and location on the file system, and the current position within the file at which data will be read or written.

So the first thing we need to do is to get a file pointer. This is done using the C function **fopen**, which takes two arguments. The first argument is the path to the file, including its name and extension. The second argument is called the *file access mode*; this is a code which indicates whether you intend to read from the file or write to it.

Let's look at an example of reading a file. Use your text editor to create a file called **input.txt** in the **/home/pi** directory on your Raspberry Pi, and type anything you like into it. Save it, and then create and run the following program:

```c
#include <stdio.h>

void main (void)
{
  FILE *fp;
  int value;

  fp = fopen ("/home/pi/input.txt", "rb");
  if (fp)
  {
    while (1)
    {
      value = fgetc (fp);
      if (value == EOF) break;
      else printf ("%c", value);
```

```
    }
    fclose (fp);
  }
}
```

First, we declare a file pointer variable called **fp**, which has the type **FILE ***. We also declare an integer which we'll use to hold the characters read in from the file.

We then create the file pointer using the command **fopen** (for 'file open'). We open the file at **/home/pi/input.txt**, and we set the mode to **"rb"**, which indicates 'read binary'. This creates the file pointer and initialises it to the beginning of the file.

We then check to see if the file pointer is non-zero; if the pointer is returned as zero, the file wasn't successfully opened. (For a read, this usually indicates that the file doesn't exist.)

If the file pointer does exist, we call the function **fgetc** (for 'file get character') in a loop; each time this function is called, it reads a single byte from the file, and then advances the file pointer to the next byte in the file. When the file pointer reaches the end of the file, it returns the special value **EOF** (for 'end of file'). So we print the value returned by **fgetc** each time until it returns **EOF**.

Once we have finished reading the file, we finish access to it by calling **fclose** (for 'file close'), which frees the file pointer and allows you to reuse it to access another file.

Note that while **fgetc** reads characters, it returns an integer; this is because the code for **EOF** falls outside the valid range of a char variable (0–255). Unless at the end of a file, **fgetc** returns an integer value which can always be treated as a char.

ALWAYS CHECK YOUR FILE POINTER

Never assume that **fopen** has worked – always check that the value it returns is a valid pointer (i.e. not zero). If you try to read from a zero pointer, you'll get random nonsense; if you write to a zero pointer, you'll probably crash the computer!

Writing a file

To write to a file, we use a file pointer in exactly the same way, but we open it in a mode for writing.

```
#include <stdio.h>

void main (void)
{
  FILE *fp;
  int value;
```

```
    fp = fopen ("/home/pi/output.txt", "wb");

    if (fp)
    {
      for (value = 48; value < 58; value++)
      {
        fputc (value, fp);
      }
      fclose (fp);
    }
  }
```

In this case, we open the file **/home/pi/output.txt** with the mode **"wb"**, which indicates 'write binary'. This opens the file for writing; if this file already exists, the contents are deleted.

We then call the function **fputc** (for 'file put character') in a loop, writing the bytes 48, 49…57 to the file. (These are the character codes for the text characters for the ten digits 0, 1…9). As before, we then close the file pointer. If you run this and then look in your home directory, you should find the file **output.txt**, containing the string 0123456789.

REMEMBER TO FCLOSE

It's easy to forget to call **fclose** on your file, but it's important to do so. On some systems, when writing to the file system, the write doesn't actually complete until **fclose** is called; if your program doesn't call **fclose**, you might find that you write to files and nothing shows up.

Formatted output

fputc is useful for writing bytes to a file, but it's an inconvenient way of writing text to a file. For this, we can use the **fprintf** function ('file print formatted').

```
#include <stdio.h>

void main (void)
{
  FILE *fp;

  fp = fopen ("/home/pi/output.txt", "wb");

  if (fp)
  {
```

```
      fprintf (fp, "This is some text.\n");
      fclose (fp);
   }
}
```

fprintf works in exactly the same way as **sprintf**, but the first argument is a file pointer rather than a string.

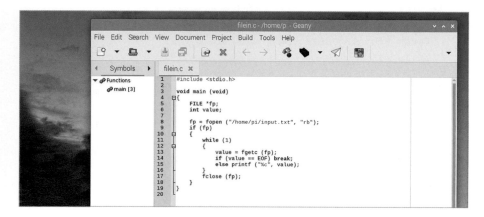

▲ Reading or writing a file requires a file pointer to be opened with **fopen**, and the resulting pointer is then used in **all** operations. Remember to close the pointer afterwards with **fclose**

READ AND WRITE THE SAME FILE

You can open a file for simultaneous reading and writing with the same pointer. Set the file access mode to **"rb+"** to read an existing file and to overwrite it; set it to **"wb+"** to create a new file and be able to read back what you've written to it; set it to **"ab+"** to open a file to both append at the end and read from it.

Moving around a file

Quite often, rather than overwriting a file, we just want to add to the end of it. To do this, open it with **fopen ("/home/pi/output.txt", "ab")**. Note that **"ab"** indicates 'append binary'. If the file exists, output will then be added after the existing file contents; if the file doesn't exist, it will be created and output will start at the beginning.

Sometimes when accessing a file, we don't necessarily want to start at the beginning. The **fseek** (for 'file seek') function can be used to reposition the file pointer within the file.

```c
#include <stdio.h>

void main (void)
{
  FILE *fp;
  int value;

  fp = fopen ("/home/pi/input.txt", "rb");
  if (fp)
  {
    fseek (fp, 10, SEEK_CUR);
    while (1)
    {
      value = fgetc (fp);
      if (value == EOF) break;
      else printf ("%c", value);
    }
    fclose (fp);
  }
}
```

The line **fseek (fp, 10, SEEK_CUR)** moves the file pointer 10 bytes ahead of the current position, so this program will print all but the first ten characters in the file. The first argument to **fseek** is the file pointer; the second is the offset by which the pointer is to move. This can be positive or negative; so **fseek (fp, -5, SEEK_CUR)** moves the pointer 5 bytes back from the current position.

The third argument to **fseek** allows you to choose a position relative to the start of the file (**SEEK_SET**) or the end of the file (**SEEK_END**) rather than the current position (**SEEK_CUR**). So **fseek (fp, 12, SEEK_SET)** positions the pointer 12 bytes ahead of the start of the file, while **fseek (fp, -17, SEEK_END)** positions it 17 bytes back from the end of the file.

CHECK THE LIBRARY

The C library offers a wide range of functions for reading and writing data from and to files; we've just looked at some of them. If you need to access a file, have a look at some of the other library functions, like **fread**, **fwrite**, **fscanf**, **fputs**, and **fgets**, to see if they are more appropriate than the basic **fputc** and **fgetc** we've used here.

Chapter 11

More about types and variables

Global variables, type definitions, enumerations, and structures

I n this chapter, we're going to look at some of the more advanced topics around the use of variables and types, including the difference between local and global variables, defining new types, and the use of enumerations and data structures.

When we've used variables in the examples in this book, we've always put them inside function definitions. These are therefore *local variables*; that is, variables which are local to those functions and have no meaning outside the function.

Global variables

C also allows *global variables*; that is, variables which are defined outside all functions. These have global *scope*, which means they can be read and written from any function within the program. Let's look at an example:

```c
#include <stdio.h>

int result;

void add (int a, int b)
{
  result = a + b;
}

void main (void)
{
  add (3, 4);
  printf ("The result is %d\n", result);
}
```

In this example, the variable **result** is global. It can therefore be read or written within both the **add** function and the **main** function; as you can see, we write a value to it in **add** and read it back in **main**, and so we don't need to return a value from **add**.

In some ways, this looks easier than passing values about all over the place, surely? So why not just do this all the time? The answer is memory. Local variables in functions are temporarily allocated space while the function is running, and the memory is freed up as soon as the function ends. But global variables are allocated space when the program starts, and that space isn't freed until the program ends; if you allocate enough of them, you can run out of memory on some systems.

There's a better way of making a lot of data available to every function, which we will come to a bit later on...

USE DIFFERENT NAMES

While it's perfectly valid to give a local variable the same name as a global variable in the same program, don't do it! If you have a global and a local with the same name, the local version is used in the function in which it is declared, and the global is used everywhere else – this can result in unexpected behaviour.

Type definitions

In chapter 2, we looked at the range of variable types in C: **char**, **int**, **float**, and so on. C also allows you to define your own types, with what is known as a *typedef*. A typedef is a line of the format **typedef <existing type> <new name>**, usually put at the start of a program. For example:

```
typedef unsigned char BYTE;
```

This defines a new type called **BYTE**, which is another name for an unsigned char. (Note that by convention, user-defined types are usually given names in capital letters. It's not compulsory, but it does help to distinguish them from variables when reading the code.)

When we say this defines a new type, what it really does is to create an alias to an existing type. This seems a bit pointless, but it can help in two ways. First, it can make it more obvious what your code is doing if you make the type names specific to your program's data. Second, by defining specific types, you can get the compiler to warn you if you use the wrong type for a function argument or variable.

There are a couple of specific cases where typedefs are particularly useful: these are enumerated types and data structures.

Enumerated types

Often, there's a use for a variable which can only take one of a few possible values. C provides a type called **enum** for this purpose, which defines an integer with a fixed set of named values.

Here's an example:

```c
#include <stdio.h>

typedef enum {
  false,
  true
} BOOLEAN;

void main (void)
{
  BOOLEAN b_var;

  b_var = false;
  if (b_var == true)
  {
    printf ("TRUE\n");
  }
  else
  {
    printf ("FALSE\n");
  }
}
```

As you can see, the named values of the enumerated type are used instead of numbers for assignments and comparisons. This can make code a lot easier to understand, and is a very good way of preventing errors, as an enumerated variable can only ever be set to a valid value.

NUMBERED ENUMS

When you create an enum, the compiler assigns a numeric value to each of the possible values. By default, it numbers the first in the list as 0 and counts up from there. You can override this by putting an equals sign after each named value and setting it to the value you want.

Structures

The other really useful thing you can do with a typedef is to use it to define a *data structure*. This is a collection of individual variables which are grouped together, allowing you to pass the structure between functions rather than the individual variables.

Here's an example:

```c
#include <stdio.h>

typedef struct {
  int inval1;
  int inval2;
  int outval;
} MY_DATA;

void add (MY_DATA *d)
{
  d->outval = d->inval1 + d->inval2;
}

void main (void)
{
  MY_DATA data;

  data.inval1 = 5;
  data.inval2 = 7;
  add (&data);

  printf ("The sum of %d and %d is %d\n", data.inval1,
      data.inval2, data.outval);
}
```

So here we use a typedef to create a data type called **MY_DATA**. The definition of the structure consists of the keyword **struct** with a list of variables enclosed by curly brackets; in this case, the structure consists of three integer variables.

NEW TYPES INSIDE STRUCTURES

A structure can contain other new types (plain types, enums, or indeed other structures); just make sure the typedefs for them occur before the typedef of the structure in which you want to include them.

The terminal shows:

```
pi@raspberrypi: ~
File  Edit  Tabs  Help
pi@raspberrypi:~ $ ./myprog
The sum of 5 ard 7 is 12
pi@raspberrypi:~ $
```

▲ An instance of the MY_DATA structure is used to pass the three integers to the **add** function

In the main function, we declare an instance of the structure as a variable called **data** of type **MY_DATA**. We then access the individual elements of the structure by giving the name of the structure variable (**data**), a full stop (**.**), and the name of the specific element. So the line `data.inval1 = 5` sets the value of the element **inval1** of **data** to 5, and so on.

The function **add** takes a pointer to a **MY_DATA** structure as its only argument; as ever, a function cannot change the values of its arguments, but can change values pointed to by its arguments, so we pass a pointer rather than the structure itself.

To access the elements of a structure from a pointer to it, we replace the full stop with an arrow made up of a minus sign and a greater than sign (**->**). So the **add** function reads the values of **inval1** and **inval2** in the structure pointed to by **d**, and then writes the result back to **outval** in the same structure; the **main** function then prints the result from the structure.

Structures are very useful if you need to pass a lot of data around between functions; they can be a lot more memory-efficient than having large numbers of global variables, as you only need to create the structure as and when you need it, rather than taking up memory all the time.

. VS ->

When accessing a structure's elements, make sure you use the right symbol. A **.** is used if your variable is an instance of the structure itself; a **->** is used if your variable is a pointer to an instance of the structure. Using the wrong one will usually give an error.

Chapter 12

Header files and the preprocessor

Splitting code up into multiple files

All the examples we've seen so far have put all the code for a program in a single C file. But once programs get big, it makes more sense to be able to split them up into separate files, grouping similar functions together. To understand how this works, we need to look in more detail at what the compiler actually does.

In all the examples so far, we've called gcc on a single source file and it has created a single executable program. This hides the fact that gcc actually does two things: first, it compiles your C source file into what's called an *object file*, and then it *links* the object file with all the library functions to create the executable. This second step is performed by a program called a *linker*; gcc actually does both jobs.

If you create a program with multiple source files, you just need to include the names of all the source files in the call to gcc. It will then create one object file for each source file, and then link all your object files together to create the executable.

There's one snag, though. If you've separated your code into separate files (usually referred to as *modules*), you'll have some files which make calls to functions in other files in order to work. These files don't find out about each other until the linker operates on them; the files are compiled individually, and the compiler will complain if you use functions in a file it doesn't know about.

We fix this using *header files*. These are files with the extension .h which hold the declarations of functions (and global variables) defined in a module, so that the compiler can be told about them when they're used by another module. We've already seen this many times; remember that line `#include <stdio.h>` at the top of the examples? That is exactly this process; it's telling the compiler that functions declared in the system header file **stdio.h** are used in this module.

KEEP NAMES CONSISTENT

While you can call header files whatever you like – there's no magic about the names – it's good practice to give the header file for the functions in a particular C file the same name as the C file itself, with a .h extension rather than .c. This makes it easier for someone reading your code to find the files where functions are defined.

Splitting code into multiple files

Let's look at an example of how this works. Create three files, two with the extension .c and one with the extension .h, as follows:

```
function.c

int add_vals (int a, int b, int c)
{
    return a + b + c;
}

function.h

extern int add_vals (int a, int b, int c);

main.c

#include <stdio.h>
#include "function.h"

void main (void)
{
    printf ("The total is %d\n", add_vals (1, 2, 3));
}
```

Put all three files in the same directory and run gcc, giving it the names of both .c files – `gcc -o myprog main.c function.c`.

The resulting program will run the **main** function from **main.c**, which calls the **add_vals** function from **function.c**.

A few things to note. First, inside the header file we declare the function with the word **extern** at the start of the declaration. This tells the compiler that this function is to be found externally to the file, i.e. in another C file.

Second, while we have always included **stdio.h** with its name between <> signs, we include **function.h** in double quotes. The <> signs tell the compiler to look for the file in the directory where the system's include files are stored; the **""** signs indicate that the file is local and is in the same directory as the .c files you're building. If you're creating your own header files, always use double quotes around the name when including them.

The preprocessor

So what does **#include** actually do? It's an instruction to the *preprocessor*, which is the first stage of compiling; it substitutes text within source files before passing them to the compiler itself. The preprocessor is controlled with what are called *directives*; these are easy to spot, as they all start with a **#** sign.

The **#include** directive instructs the preprocessor to replace the line with the file which it's including. So in our example above, the line **#include "function.h"** in the .c file gets replaced with the contents of the file **function.h**, meaning that what's passed to the compiler looks like:

```
#include <stdio.h>
extern int add_vals (int a, int b, int c);

void main (void)
{
   printf ("The total is %d\n", add_vals (1, 2, 3));
}
```

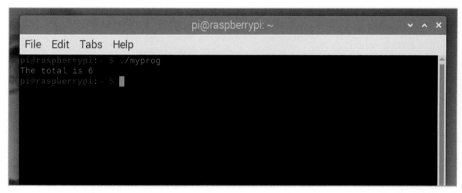

▲ The add_vals function is called from the main function – the linker connects the call from main.c to the function definition in function.c

> **DON'T #INCLUDE C FILES**
>
> **#include** will work on any file; it just substitutes the include line with the contents of the file. Occasionally you'll see this being abused; some programmers bypass the use of header files by just including the other C files themselves. While this does work, it's poor practice; don't be tempted to try it!

#define

Another useful directive is **#define**, which can be used to define constant values. Look at this example:

```c
#include <stdio.h>

#define PI 3.14159

void main (void)
{
   float rad = 3;
   float circ = rad * 2 * PI;
   float area = rad * rad * PI;
   printf ("The circumference of a circle radius %f is %f\n",
       rad, circ);
   printf ("The area of a circle radius %f is %f\n", rad, area);
}
```

The directive **#define** is used to set the value of pi. The important thing to remember is that **PI** isn't a variable; it's text that will be substituted by the preprocessor. The **#define** line tells the preprocessor to go through the file and replace every instance of the text **PI** with the digits 3.14159 before passing it to the compiler. So a line which does something like **PI = 5;** will cause an error; the compiler will see the meaningless statement **3.14159 = 5;**.

Why is this useful? Why not just declare a float variable called **PI** and set it to 3.14159? A floating-point variable requires allocating memory in which to store it; using **#define** saves that memory, which is useful if memory is limited.

You can also **#define** functions:

```c
#include <stdio.h>
#define ADD(a,b) (a+b)
```

```
void main (void)
{
  printf ("The sum of %d and %d is %d\n", 5, 2, ADD(5,2));
  printf ("The sum of %d and %d is %d\n", 3, 7, ADD(3,7));
}
```

Again, this does a text substitution; whenever **ADD(a,b)** appears in the code, it's replaced by **(a+b)**, with the values of **a** and **b** replaced by the arguments to **ADD**.

The preprocessor can also evaluate conditions with the **#if** directive:

```
#include <stdio.h>

void main (void)
{
#if 0
  printf ("Some code\n");
#else
  printf ("Some other code\n");
#endif
}
```

With a 0 after the **#if**, the code between the **#if** and the **#else** doesn't get called, but the code between the **#else** and the **#endif** does. If you change the value after the **#if** to a 1, the code between the **#if** and the **#else** does get called, but the code between the **#else** and the **#endif** doesn't. This is a really useful trick to temporarily remove or replace a piece of code when you're debugging.

#DEFINES FOR TEXT

If you use #define for text strings, they should be enclosed in double quotes, otherwise the replaced text will end at the first space. So use #define MY_TEXT "This is some text to replace." The double quotes are included in the replacement, so you can then just call printf (MY_TEXT);

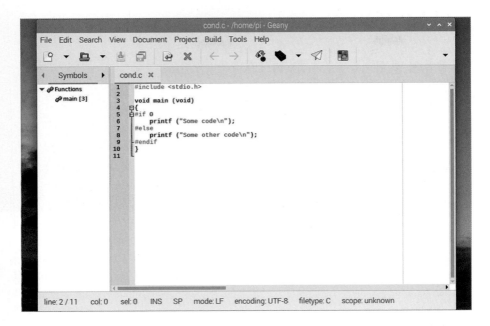

The most common use of `#if` is for temporarily removing code – just wrap it between an `#if` 0 and an `#endif`. The `#else` is optional, but sometimes you want to substitute the code you've removed with different code

Chapter 13

Introduction to GTK

Now you have a grounding in C programming, you are ready to start creating GUIs

S o far in this book, we've learnt the basics of the C language, and seen how to use it to write text-only programs you run at the command line. Looking at the keywords and library functions that we've seen so far, it isn't obvious how you can create everything required for a full graphical user interface – desktop, windows, icons, mouse pointer, and so on – with them.

It is entirely possible to do so in C, but to be honest, it would be incredibly long-winded and time-consuming. You need to find the screen buffer in memory – the part of memory that represents the pixels which make up the desktop on the screen – and then write new pixels to it for each window; you then have to write even more pixels to it to show where the mouse cursor is. You then have to monitor when the user moves the mouse, and redraw the pointer each time, and then when the user clicks the mouse button, you have to work out where on the screen the pointer is and whether it is on top of a window, and so on...

Funnily enough, that isn't how it's usually done in practice – life is too short! Most of this functionality has already been written for you. Windowing systems like X provide most of the underlying features, and then user interface libraries provide a convenient means of creating GUI applications which work with the likes of X; all you need to do is choose a suitable user interface library, and use the predefined functions in it in your C program.

There are lots of user interface libraries available; some are designed to work with a particular desktop environment like Windows or macOS, while others are cross-platform and can work in a choice of desktop environments. The one which is used most often in the Raspberry Pi Desktop included with Raspberry Pi OS is called GTK, and that's the one we are going to look at in this book.

What is GTK?

GTK (formerly known as GTK+) is short for 'GIMP ToolKit'. Its website (**gtk.org**) describes it as "a multi-platform toolkit for creating graphical user interfaces", and it was originally written to provide the user interface elements used to create the GIMP picture-editing program.

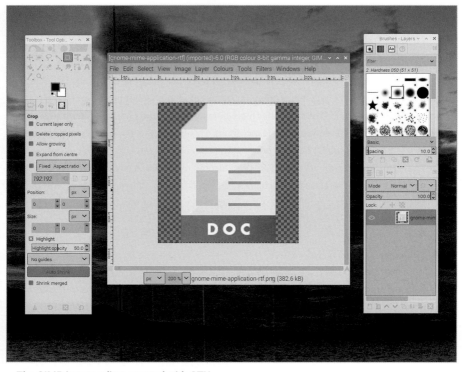

▲ The GIMP image editor, created with GTK

It has grown beyond that into a general user interface toolkit, and is now one of the most widely used user interface libraries on the Linux desktop.

The fundamental building blocks of GTK projects are called *widgets*. Everything you see on the screen – a window, a button, a label – is a widget. The GTK library does all the work required in creating widgets – all you need to do is to tell it what widgets you want, whereabouts you want to put them, and what you want them to do, and GTK will manage everything else for you.

To give you an idea of what 'manage everything else' means, imagine the situation described above where you are manually creating a window by drawing pixels by writing data to the screen buffer. If the user clicks on the window title bar and drags it to another place on the screen, you have to detect that the mouse has been clicked, you have to track that it is being moved, and you have to redraw the window at each point as it moves, restoring what was underneath it in the areas from where it has moved. Just dragging a window would be hundreds of lines of code – but with GTK, you create a 'window' widget (with a single line of code) and all of that is taken care of for you.

Libraries like GTK therefore make the creation of rich graphical user interfaces relatively easy, and you may be surprised by just how little code you need to write to get something working.

GTK versions

One thing worth mentioning at this point is that there are several versions of GTK in use. The current version is GTK 4, and this is still under active development – it changes quite a bit between releases.

For this reason, many people prefer to use one of the older versions. Some say that it is always better to use the latest and greatest version of anything, but more cautious old engineers (like the author...) tend to prefer the older version that has had a lot more testing and with which people have stopped fiddling about! This is why the 'bullseye' version of the Raspberry Pi Desktop uses GTK 3, and why it is the version covered in this book

The examples in this book all use GTK 3. While some of this code would also run correctly under GTK 2 or GTK 4, there are parts which would need to be modified to work on different versions of GTK, and these modifications are outside the scope of this book

A note on theming

One of the powerful features of GTK is *theming*. The appearance of every widget in GTK can be customised in pretty much every detail, from the colour of the text to the shape of the corners on a button. This customisation is completely separate from the actual coding of a GTK application; instead, the appearance of widgets is controlled by the current theme which is in use on the system on which the GTK applications are running.

Creating a theme is beyond the scope of this book – it's quite a complicated and fiddly procedure. All the example screenshots in this book were taken from a Raspberry Pi running the Raspberry Pi Desktop environment, which uses a custom theme called PiXflat. If you are working with GTK on a different computer with a different theme, your widgets may look slightly different from those pictured, but the code you write will be the same.

Chapter 14

Your first GTK program

Start coding in C with the GTK library and create your first simple GUI application

L et's create a simple GTK program. Open your favourite text editor, and write the following.

```
#include <gtk/gtk.h>

int main (int argc, char *argv[])
{
  gtk_init (&argc, &argv);
  GtkWidget *win = gtk_window_new (GTK_WINDOW_TOPLEVEL);
  gtk_widget_show (win);
  gtk_main ();
  return 0;
}
```

I told you you didn't need much code! Let's look at that line-by-line before we try to run it.

```
#include <gtk/gtk.h>
```

This is an instruction to the preprocessor to tell it that we are writing a GTK program, and to load the GTK header files. Without this, the compiler won't recognise any of the GTK library functions that we are going to use.

```
int main (int argc, char *argv[])
```

This is the standard starting point of a C program – a **main** function with some arguments and a return value.

```
  gtk_init (&argc, &argv);
```

This is our first piece of GTK code. You need to call **gtk_init** at the start of every GTK program – this initialises all the internal variables used by the GTK library and sets it up ready to use. (Note that any command-line arguments supplied to the program are passed on to the GTK library via the arguments to this function.)

```
GtkWidget *win = gtk_window_new (GTK_WINDOW_TOPLEVEL);
```

This creates a widget of type GtkWindow. For every type of widget in GTK, there is a **_new** function which creates an instance of that widget and returns a pointer to it.

```
gtk_widget_show (win);
```

This tells GTK to show the widget we have just created. The previous line created the widget in a hidden state; widgets can only be seen if they are unhidden with a **_show** call like this.

```
gtk_main ();
```

The **gtk_main** call runs the *main loop* of GTK; this effectively hands control of the program to GTK itself, which then processes any user events like button pushes to control the user interface you have created.

```
return 0;
```

Formally, as this is a C program with the **main** function returning an integer value, we need to return a value. However, this is largely pointless with a GUI program where the command line, and hence any return value, is usually never seen anyway; it's included here for completeness, but to save space, it won't be in any other examples in this book.

That's really all there is to it – that's the simplest GTK program which will do something sensible. Type it in using your favourite editor and save it as **gtktest.c**. Now we need to build and run it...

Building a GTK program

If we're writing a standard command-line C program, we can just use the gcc compiler to build our source file – **gcc gtktest.c** would produce an executable file. However, things are not quite so simple if we are using an external library like GTK.

First we need to make sure that the relevant GTK libraries are installed. To do this, type **sudo apt-get install libgtk-3-dev** into a terminal window and answer yes to any prompts – this installs the developer libraries for GTK 3.

Now we need to tell the compiler where to find the GTK header files, and also we need to tell the linker that we want the program linked with the GTK library files, otherwise all the 'GTK-ness' we want to use will be unavailable.

There is a utility called pkg-config that helps here. pkg-config is a tool which generates the arguments required by gcc in order to use additional libraries. Try typing **pkg-config –cflags –libs gtk+-3.0** at the command line and look at the output. You'll see a list of strings – those which start **-I/** are the directories where the GTK include files are stored, and those which start **-l** are the names of the GTK library files.

▲ The output of pkg-config is a long list of the flags and libraries that need to be passed to the compiler to build a GTK program

All of these need to be added to the gcc command line in order to build our GTK program, so the pkg-config command is enclosed within back-ticks (`), like so:

```
gcc gtktest.c `pkg-config –cflags –libs gtk+-3.0` -o gtktest
```

If you run this, you should end up with an executable file called **gtktest**. Run this by typing:

```
./gtktest
```

…and see what happens.

▲ Your first GTK window

You should see a small grey square window open somewhere on your desktop; it won't do much, but you can drag it around and minimise and maximise it. If you press the X in the top-right corner, the window closes, but if you look in the terminal window from which you ran gtktest, you'll see the program is still running. This is because closing a window doesn't terminate the **gtk_main** function, which will carry on running until you hit **CTRL+C** in the terminal window.

Congratulations! You've just created your first GUI application with GTK. In the next chapter, we'll put something onto that empty window.

Chapter 15
Buttons

Make your empty window more interesting
and interactive by adding a button

T he simple program we looked at in the previous chapter draws a window on the
screen, but it looks rather bare. There's also that problem that closing the window
with the X button leaves the program still running. We're going to fix both of those by
adding a button to close the window.

A button is another standard GTK widget, and it supports all the features you'd expect – you
can have a label on it; you can see its appearance change when you click it; you can activate it
with a keyboard shortcut; you can even disable it temporarily and grey it out.

The first thing to do is to add the button to the window. When we've done that, we can look
at making it do something useful.

Modify the code for the previous example as follows:

```
#include <gtk/gtk.h>

void main (int argc, char *argv[])
{
  gtk_init (&argc, &argv);
  GtkWidget *win = gtk_window_new (GTK_WINDOW_TOPLEVEL);
  GtkWidget *btn = gtk_button_new_with_label ("Close window");
  gtk_container_add (GTK_CONTAINER (win), btn);
  gtk_widget_show_all (win);
  gtk_main ();
}
```

Let's look at the changes:

```
GtkWidget *btn = gtk_button_new_with_label ("Close window");
```

This creates a GtkButton widget. There is a standard **gtk_button_new** function, but using
this version, **gtk_button_new_with_label**, allows us to add a text label to the button at
the same time as we create it.

```
gtk_container_add (GTK_CONTAINER (win), btn);
```

The **gtk_container_add** function places the button inside the window.

```
gtk_widget_show_all (win);
```

Finally, the call to **gtk_widget_show** is replaced with a call to **gtk_widget_show_all** – this tells GTK to show both the named widget and any widgets it contains. If this line weren't changed, the window would be shown, but the button would remain hidden.

If you now build and run the code, you'll find that you get a (smaller) window with a button labelled 'Close window' displayed on it:

▲ The window with a button on it

Containers

In the example, we use the line:

```
gtk_container_add (GTK_CONTAINER (win), btn);
```

...to put the button into the window.

As you've probably noticed, each function call in GTK starts with the prefix **gtk_**, which is then followed by the name of the widget type upon which it operates – so **gtk_window_new** creates a widget of type GtkWindow. This function call, therefore, operates on widgets of type GtkContainer, but we are using it on **win**, which is a GtkWindow. How does that work?

There is a hierarchy of widget types within GTK, and a widget type *inherits* the properties of its *parents* within the hierarchy; that widget type can be described as a *child* of the widget types above it in the hierarchy.

Because GtkContainer is one of the parents of GtkWindow, you can use **gtk_container_** functions on GtkWindow widgets. Many widgets have GtkContainer as a parent, because putting one widget inside another like this is something we need to do quite often.

You will notice that when **win** is supplied as an argument to the **gtk_container_add** function, it is wrapped inside the **GTK_CONTAINER()** function – this *casts* the argument to a variable of type **GTK_CONTAINER**; in other words, it tells the function call to treat this reference to a GtkWindow as a GtkContainer. The code will still work if this function isn't included, but the compiler will complain! (GTK includes a **GTK_** function for every type of widget, as it is quite common to need to cast a widget to a different type.)

So what this line does is to tell GTK to treat the GtkWindow widget **win** as a GtkContainer, and to put the button widget **btn** into it.

Signals

If you run the application, you can click the button with the mouse, and it will highlight to show that it has been clicked; you can also hit the **ENTER** key on the keyboard to do the same thing – this button behaves exactly like the buttons we are used to seeing in applications, but it still doesn't actually do anything useful. The next step is to fix that.

The way to do that is to connect a *handler* function to the *signal* generated when the button is clicked.

Here's the code with a handler added:

```
#include <gtk/gtk.h>

void end_program (GtkWidget *wid, gpointer ptr)
{
    gtk_main_quit ();
}

void main (int argc, char *argv[])
{
  gtk_init (&argc, &argv);
  GtkWidget *win = gtk_window_new (GTK_WINDOW_TOPLEVEL);
  GtkWidget *btn = gtk_button_new_with_label ("Close window");
  g_signal_connect (btn, "clicked", G_CALLBACK (end_program),
      NULL);
  gtk_container_add (GTK_CONTAINER (win), btn);
  gtk_widget_show_all (win);
  gtk_main ();
}
```

The handler function, otherwise known as a *callback*, is called **end_program**, and all it does is to call the GTK function **gtk_main_quit** – as you'd expect from the name, this function exits the loop within **gtk_main** and allows the program to end.

```
    g_signal_connect (btn, "clicked", G_CALLBACK (end_program),
        NULL);
```

This line connects the handler (**end_program**) to the signal called **clicked**, which is emitted by a button widget when the mouse is clicked on it. We use the **GTK_CALLBACK** function to make sure the compiler knows that the **end_program** function is a valid callback.

Signals are used a lot in GTK; all widgets can generate signals under various circumstances – mostly when interacted with by the user, but also when certain system events occur. Each type of widget has a set of signals it can generate; the **g_signal_connect** function is used to 'connect' a handler function to them, meaning it will be called when the signal is generated.

Handling signals is one of the most important jobs of the main loop which runs inside **gtk_main** – if a signal is generated, code in the main loop checks to see if there is a handler associated with that signal, and calls the handler if so.

Try building and running the new code. We now have a button on the window as before, but when we click the button, the window closes and, importantly, the program exits as well.

This still isn't perfect, though – if we click the X at the top right, the window closes but the program doesn't exit. Let's fix that.

The way we do this is to connect another handler to the signal generated when that X is clicked. The name of this signal is **delete_event**, and it is generated from the window widget. So we need to connect the same handler to that event as well:

```
g_signal_connect (win, "delete_event", G_CALLBACK (end_program),
    NULL);
```

Note that we connect to **win** rather than to **btn** this time – the **delete_event** signal is created by the window widget rather than the button. Now if the window is closed by clicking the X, the **delete_event** signal causes the **end_program** handler to be called and the main loop then exits.

We've now got a GTK application that opens and closes cleanly, but it still doesn't do anything else. So in the next chapter, we'll make it do something more useful.

Chapter 16
Labels and layout

Use a box widget to add a text label to your window,
and then create a button push counter

We're going to add another button to the window, and display a count of the number of times the button is pressed. (All I said was that it would be *more* useful than the previous example; I didn't say it would be useful for anything people might actually want to do!)

Labels

For displaying text on a window, we use a widget called a GtkLabel – a label is any piece of text which can't be edited by the user. (The button we added in the previous example contains a label widget, which displays the name we gave the button in the `gtk_button_new_with_label` call.)

You can create a label with text already in it, or you can create a blank label and add text to it later on; you can also change the existing text in a label whenever you like.

Here's the code to add a label to our window:

```
#include <gtk/gtk.h>

void end_program (GtkWidget *wid, gpointer ptr)
{
    gtk_main_quit ();
}

void main (int argc, char *argv[])
{
  gtk_init (&argc, &argv);
  GtkWidget *win = gtk_window_new (GTK_WINDOW_TOPLEVEL);
  GtkWidget *btn = gtk_button_new_with_label ("Close window");
  g_signal_connect (btn, "clicked", G_CALLBACK (end_program),
      NULL);
  g_signal_connect (win, "delete_event", G_CALLBACK (end_program),
      NULL);
  gtk_container_add (GTK_CONTAINER (win), btn);
```

```
GtkWidget *lbl = gtk_label_new ("My label");
gtk_container_add (GTK_CONTAINER (win), lbl);
gtk_widget_show_all (win);
gtk_main ();
}
```

Let's look at the new code:

```
GtkWidget *lbl = gtk_label_new ("My label");
```

This creates a GtkLabel called **lbl**, with the text 'My label' in it. We then call another **gtk_container_add** to add the label to the window. Build and run the code, and see what happens.

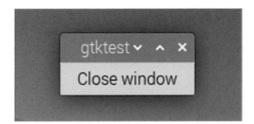

▲ A button, but no label...

Ah. A window with a button, but no label. What's gone wrong? Well, if you look at the terminal window, you can get a clue – you should see an error message telling you that a GtkWindow can only contain one widget at a time, and that this one already contains a GtkButton.

So you can only put one widget into a window, but we want to have two – a button and a label; that's not going to work. Unless...

Boxes

A UI toolkit that only allowed you to put one thing at a time on a window would be a bit limited! So while a window can only contain one widget, GTK has several widgets which can be used to hold sets of other widgets. The two most useful ones are boxes and grids – we'll stick to boxes for now, as they are easier to use.

A box widget can have one of two orientations, either horizontal or vertical, depending on how the widgets you put into the box are to be arranged. A box widget can hold an unlimited number of other widgets, but appears to its parent as a single widget, so can be used to put multiple widgets into a window.

We are going to use a GtkBox with vertical orientation for this example, so modify the code as follows:

```
#include <gtk/gtk.h>

void end_program (GtkWidget *wid, gpointer ptr)
{
    gtk_main_quit ();
}

void main (int argc, char *argv[])
{
    gtk_init (&argc, &argv);
    GtkWidget *win = gtk_window_new (GTK_WINDOW_TOPLEVEL);
    GtkWidget *btn = gtk_button_new_with_label ("Close window");
    g_signal_connect (btn, "clicked", G_CALLBACK (end_program),
        NULL);
    g_signal_connect (win, "delete_event", G_CALLBACK (end_program),
        NULL);
    GtkWidget *lbl = gtk_label_new ("My label");
    GtkWidget *box = gtk_box_new (GTK_ORIENTATION_VERTICAL, 5);
    gtk_box_pack_start (GTK_BOX (box), lbl, TRUE, TRUE, 0);
    gtk_box_pack_start (GTK_BOX (box), btn, TRUE, TRUE, 0);
    gtk_container_add (GTK_CONTAINER (win), box);
    gtk_widget_show_all (win);
    gtk_main ();
}
```

Let's look at the changes line-by-line:

```
GtkWidget *box = gtk_box_new (GTK_ORIENTATION_VERTICAL, 5);
```

This creates a new GtkBox widget. The two parameters to the call are the orientation of the box – either horizontal or vertical – and the spacing in pixels between the widgets it holds. So in this case, the widgets in the box will be oriented vertically – above and below each other – and there will be a gap of 5 pixels between the two widgets we are putting into it.

```
gtk_box_pack_start (GTK_BOX (box), lbl, TRUE, TRUE, 0);
gtk_box_pack_start (GTK_BOX (box), btn, TRUE, TRUE, 0);
```

The **gtk_box_pack_start** function puts a widget into a box. Widgets are added in the order that calls to this function are made, and the **_start** at the end indicates that widgets are placed in the box from the 'start' end, which is the top of a vertical box or the left-hand side of a horizontal box. (There is also a **gtk_box_pack_end** function, which adds widgets from the bottom or right-hand sides.)

The function takes five arguments; the first is the name of the box we are packing the widgets into, and the second is the widget we want to put into the box. The remaining three arguments control how the widget is positioned in the box – we'll look at this later on.

```
gtk_container_add (GTK_CONTAINER (win), box);
```

Finally, we add the box to the window itself – this means that the window only holds one widget, the box, and so won't complain about holding too many widgets.

If you now build and run this, you should see a window like the following:

▲ A GtkLabel and a GtkButton

Now we have a window containing the controls we need, let's get back to creating our button push counter. Here's the code:

```
#include <gtk/gtk.h>

int count = 0;

void end_program (GtkWidget *wid, gpointer ptr)
{
    gtk_main_quit ();
}

void count_button (GtkWidget *wid, gpointer ptr)
{
    char buffer[30];
    count++;
    sprintf (buffer, "Button pressed %d times", count);
    gtk_label_set_text (GTK_LABEL (ptr), buffer);
}
```

```c
void main (int argc, char *argv[])
{
  gtk_init (&argc, &argv);

  GtkWidget *win = gtk_window_new (GTK_WINDOW_TOPLEVEL);
  GtkWidget *btn = gtk_button_new_with_label ("Close window");
  g_signal_connect (btn, "clicked", G_CALLBACK (end_program),
      NULL);
  g_signal_connect (win, "delete_event", G_CALLBACK (end_program),
      NULL);

  GtkWidget *lbl = gtk_label_new ("My label");

  GtkWidget *btn2 = gtk_button_new_with_label ("Count button");
  g_signal_connect (btn2, "clicked", G_CALLBACK (count_button), lbl);

  GtkWidget *box = gtk_box_new (GTK_ORIENTATION_VERTICAL, 5);
  gtk_box_pack_start (GTK_BOX (box), btn2, TRUE, TRUE, 0);
  gtk_box_pack_start (GTK_BOX (box), lbl, TRUE, TRUE, 0);
  gtk_box_pack_start (GTK_BOX (box), btn, TRUE, TRUE, 0);
  gtk_container_add (GTK_CONTAINER (win), box);
  gtk_widget_show_all (win);
  gtk_main ();
}
```

We've added a new button, **btn2**, and a new handler callback function, **count_button**, which has been connected to the **clicked** signal on the new button.

```c
g_signal_connect (btn2, "clicked", G_CALLBACK (count_button), lbl);
```

Note that whenever we have used **g_signal_connect** before, the last argument has been **NULL**, but in this case it is **lbl**. The final argument of this function is a pointer − it can be a pointer to anything which the handler might need to use. If you look at the arguments to the handler function, they are:

```c
void count_button (GtkWidget *wid, gpointer ptr)
```

The first argument of a handler for any signal is a pointer to the widget that generated the signal. Different signals have different numbers of arguments in their handler functions, but they all have a general-purpose pointer as the last argument, and this receives the pointer that is supplied as the last argument to the **g_signal_connect** call.

In this case, we need to update the text in the GtkLabel, so the handler needs access to a pointer to the label, and the general-purpose pointer is a convenient way of doing this. So we pass the **lbl** pointer into **g_signal_connect**, and in the handler we cast this pointer back to a GtkLabel so we can use it in the **gtk_label_set_text** function, which updates the text in the label:

```
gtk_label_set_text (GTK_LABEL (ptr), buffer);
```

Sometimes we need to pass more than one reference to something to a handler function; there are various ways around this like the use of structures or global variables, but for simple cases like this, the general-purpose pointer works well.

If you now build and run the code, you should see a window which looks like this:

▲ The button counting application before a button is pressed...

When you click on 'Count button', the text in the label should update on each click, like this:

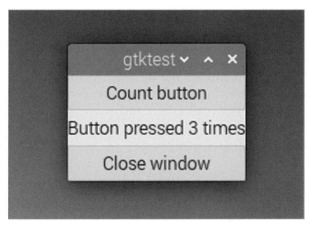

▲ ...and after the 'Count button' has been pressed three times

Chapter 17

More advanced layout

Learn how to expand your window, and position and resize buttons automatically

We mentioned in the previous chapter that boxes can be either horizontal or vertical. Just to see the difference, try changing the line:

```
GtkWidget *box = gtk_box_new (GTK_ORIENTATION_VERTICAL, 5);
```

...to:

```
GtkWidget *box = gtk_box_new (GTK_ORIENTATION_HORIZONTAL, 5);
```

...and rebuild – you should then see the following:

▲ The effect of setting the orientation of a GtkBox to horizontal instead of vertical

This demonstrates the effect of changing the orientation of a GtkBox – it just changes the direction in which the widgets are laid out.

But what about those other arguments to **gtk_box_pack_start** that we glossed over earlier? These are designed to allow you to move things around within boxes and to give you more control over exactly where things end up within the window.

In the windows we have seen so far, this doesn't seem particularly useful, as the button and label both take up as much space as they need but no more. But GTK windows can usually be resized – the user can grab a corner of a window and stretch it to an arbitrary size in each dimension. GTK tries to resize windows and widgets intelligently so that things grow and shrink in proportion to each other; these additional arguments let you control what happens to the widgets when the window size changes.

The third argument to **gtk_box_pack_start** is called **expand**. If set to **TRUE**, then when a window is enlarged, the amount of space allocated for this widget is enlarged in proportion. If set to **FALSE**, the amount of space allocated for this widget is never more than the minimum it requires.

The fourth argument is called **fill**. This has no effect if **expand** is set to **FALSE**, but if **expand** is set to **TRUE**, it controls whether or not it is the space allocated to the widget or the widget itself which grows. If **expand** is **TRUE** and **fill** is **FALSE**, the widget itself stays the same size, but the space around it grows; if both **expand** and **fill** are **TRUE**, the widget itself grows to fill the increased space.

That is somewhat hard to follow when written down, but a few examples will help to get it straight. Change the orientation of the GtkBox back to **GTK_ORIENTATION_VERTICAL**, and then set both **expand** and **fill** for all three **gtk_box_pack_start** calls in the example above to **FALSE**. If you then resize the window, the label and two buttons will all stay the same height, at the top of the window:

▲ The layout with **expand** and **fill** both set to **FALSE** for all widgets

Now try the same thing, but change the **expand** parameter in the **gtk_box_pack_start** for **btn** to **TRUE**:

▲ The layout with **expand** set to **TRUE** and `fill` set to **FALSE** for the 'Close window' button

The button now moves down the window to fit in the middle of the increased space; the extra space has been allocated to the button, but the button itself is the same size.

Finally, try changing both **expand** and `fill` to **TRUE** for **btn** to see a result like the image overleaf.

▲ The layout with both **expand** and `fill` set to TRUE for the 'Close window' button

Enlarging the window now causes the whole button to fill the extra space.

We can see that these parameters only affect the vertical size of the widgets; this is because the GtkBox they are inside has its orientation set to vertical. If we want to control the horizontal size of the widgets as well, we need to create a GtkBox with vertical orientation which contains a set of GtkBoxes, each with horizontal orientation, which are then used to contain the widgets themselves.

The final argument in the call to `gtk_box_pack_start` is called **padding** – this is the amount of free space (in pixels) which is inserted at either end of this widget; this is in addition to the `spacing` which was requested between all widgets in the `gtk_box_new` call.

By careful tweaking of **expand**, `fill`, and **padding** parameters, you can create a window which displays all its widgets tidily and resizes exactly as you expect.

Grids

You might be wondering how you put, say, four items in a window with two on each of two lines. Well, it is perfectly acceptable to put a GtkBox with horizontal orientation as one of the items inside a GtkBox with vertical orientation, or vice versa. It's even acceptable to put one box with horizontal orientation inside another box with horizontal orientation (but it's generally a bit pointless). Using a combination of nested GtkBoxes of both orientations, you can lay out all the widgets in a window the way you want them.

While nesting GtkBoxes works perfectly well for laying out widgets in two dimensions, and actually gives you the best control over how they appear, there is a simpler alternative: the GtkGrid widget. A GtkGrid is a two-dimensional box, in which widgets can be located at various row and column co-ordinates.

This is actually not as flexible as using nested GtkBoxes, because every widget has to be aligned in both a row and a column – this means that any row is always at least as high as the tallest widget anywhere in it, and any column is always at least as wide as the widest widget anywhere in it; this can lead to a lot of wasted space. But quite often a simple arrangement like this is all that is needed, so a GtkGrid works fine.

Here are the changes to our example if we use a GtkGrid to position the label and buttons:

```c
void main (int argc, char *argv[])
{
  gtk_init (&argc, &argv);

  GtkWidget *win = gtk_window_new (GTK_WINDOW_TOPLEVEL);
  GtkWidget *btn = gtk_button_new_with_label ("Close window");
  g_signal_connect (btn, "clicked", G_CALLBACK (end_program),
      NULL);
  g_signal_connect (win, "delete_event", G_CALLBACK (end_program),
      NULL);

  GtkWidget *lbl = gtk_label_new ("My label");

  GtkWidget *btn2 = gtk_button_new_with_label ("Count button");
  g_signal_connect (btn2, "clicked", G_CALLBACK (count_button),
      lbl);

  GtkWidget *grd = gtk_grid_new ();
  gtk_grid_attach (GTK_GRID (grd), lbl, 0, 0, 1, 1);
  gtk_grid_attach (GTK_GRID (grd), btn2, 1, 0, 1, 1);
  gtk_grid_attach (GTK_GRID (grd), btn, 0, 1, 2, 1);
  gtk_container_add (GTK_CONTAINER (win), grd);
  gtk_widget_show_all (win);
  gtk_main ();
}
```

We create a new GtkGrid widget with:

```
GtkWidget *grd = gtk_grid_new ();
```

To insert a widget into the grid, we use:

```
gtk_grid_attach (GTK_GRID (grd), lbl, 0, 0, 1, 1);
```

We pass as arguments the names of the grid and the widget we are putting into it. The following numbers, in order, are the x and y co-ordinates where the widget is attached to the grid, and then its width and height in grid squares.

So this positions the widget in the first column − at x position 0 with a width of 1 column − and in the first row − at y position 0 with a height of 1 row.

Note that you can spread a widget across multiple rows and/or columns, as in how **btn** is placed:

```
gtk_grid_attach (GTK_GRID (grd), btn, 0, 1, 2, 1);
```

In this case, the widget spans the first and second columns, because it is located at an x position of 0 with a width of 2.

If you build and run this code, you'll end up with a window that looks like the one below.

Note that the 'Close window' button spans both columns of the table, as described above.

▲ A GtkGrid allows widgets to be aligned in rows and columns

Chapter 18
GUI user input

Enable users to enter text, and to select options using check and radio buttons

We've seen how we can display text on a window using a label, but what about if we want to read in some text that the user has typed? GTK provides the GtkTextEntry widget for this.

Text entry

Modify the example code above to add a new cell to the grid with a GtkTextEntry widget, like so:

```
#include <gtk/gtk.h>

GtkWidget *txt;

void end_program (GtkWidget *wid, gpointer ptr)
{
  gtk_main_quit ();
}

void copy_text (GtkWidget *wid, gpointer ptr)
{
  const char *input = gtk_entry_get_text (GTK_ENTRY (txt));
  gtk_label_set_text (GTK_LABEL (ptr), input);
}

void main (int argc, char *argv[])
{
  gtk_init (&argc, &argv);

  GtkWidget *win = gtk_window_new (GTK_WINDOW_TOPLEVEL);
  GtkWidget *btn = gtk_button_new_with_label ("Close window");
  g_signal_connect (btn, "clicked", G_CALLBACK (end_program),
      NULL);
  g_signal_connect (win, "delete_event", G_CALLBACK (end_program),
      NULL);
```

```
GtkWidget *lbl = gtk_label_new ("My label");

GtkWidget *btn2 = gtk_button_new_with_label ("Copy button");
g_signal_connect (btn2, "clicked", G_CALLBACK (copy_text), lbl);

txt = gtk_entry_new ();

GtkWidget *grd = gtk_grid_new ();
gtk_grid_attach (GTK_GRID (grd), lbl, 0, 0, 1, 1);
gtk_grid_attach (GTK_GRID (grd), btn2, 1, 0, 1, 1);
gtk_grid_attach (GTK_GRID (grd), btn, 0, 1, 1, 1);
gtk_grid_attach (GTK_GRID (grd), txt, 1, 1, 1, 1);
gtk_container_add (GTK_CONTAINER (win), grd);
gtk_widget_show_all (win);
gtk_main ();
}
```

In this example, we declare a pointer to the GtkTextEntry widget, **txt**, as a global variable. This is because we need to access it from a button handler, which also needs to access the GtkLabel widget. We previously used the general-purpose pointer in the **g_signal_connect** function to pass widget information to a handler, but in this case, the handler needs access to two separate widgets, and we've only got one pointer. (There are ways of using a single pointer for this, but using a global variable is a lot easier to understand.)

We've added a new function, **copy_text** – this uses the function **gtk_entry_get_text** to get a pointer to the text buffer used by the GtkEntry widget; this stores whatever the user has typed into the entry box. Note that the pointer to this buffer of chars is declared with the modifier **const** – this indicates a variable that cannot be changed by the programmer. We then pass this buffer to **gtk_label_set_text**, which copies the contents of the GtkEntry to the GtkLabel.

Finally, we've created the GtkEntry itself with **gtk_entry_new**, and added it to the grid. (Note we've also reduced the width of **btn** so that it only takes up one cell of the grid rather than two, so as to give enough space for the GtkEntry.)

Build the code and run it; try typing something into the entry box and pressing the 'Copy button' to see what happens.

▲ A GtkEntry added to the bottom right of the grid

Spin buttons

There are various other ways for the user to enter data. Quite often they need to select one of a number of options, rather than being given a box and asked to type into it. GTK provides a number of widgets for this purpose; one, which is closely related to the GtkEntry, is the GtkSpinButton.

A spin button is used to enter a numeric value in a certain range. You specify the minimum and maximum values, and by how much the value should change on each press of the button. This gives a text entry control – which the user can still type into – with an easy way of changing the value. If the user does type in a value which is outside the limits you set, it is automatically rounded to the closest value within the limits when you try to read it.

We only need to change one line to convert the GtkEntry to a GtkSpinButton in our example above. Replace:

```
txt = gtk_entry_new ();
```

...with:

```
GtkAdjustment *adj = gtk_adjustment_new (0, -10, 10, 1, 0, 0);
txt = gtk_spin_button_new (adj, 0, 0);
```

This changes **txt** from a GtkEntry to a GtkSpinButton. We can see that one of the arguments to the **gtk_spin_button_new** function is something called a GtkAdjustment – what's that?

A GtkAdjustment is used to set the range of values that a spin button (and a few other widgets with similar behaviour) can take. So the **gtk_adjustment_new** function takes arguments which specify, in order, the default value (0 in this case), the minimum value (-10), the maximum value (10) and the step size (1). (The last two arguments specify 'page' increments, which are used in some controls where there are two different sets of buttons to change the values – a spin button doesn't use these, so they can just be set to zero.)

The GtkAdjustment is passed as an argument to the **gtk_spin_button_new** function. The other two arguments are the climb rate – how fast the value changes when the button is held down – and the number of decimal places to be shown on the value.

▲ A GtkSpinButton instead of the GtkEntry

Build and run the new version of the code; the text entry box now has two buttons labelled with a plus and a minus at the right-hand side; these can be used to change the value. You can still type into the box; if you type a value that isn't a number, or is outside the range specified in the GtkAdjustment, it will be corrected to a value within the range when one of these buttons – or 'Copy button' – is pressed.

Toggle buttons

One useful way to get input from the user is by the use of buttons to select an option. GTK offers several widgets for this purpose; two of the more useful are *check buttons* – boxes that can be ticked or unticked – and *radio buttons* – selectors in which only one member of a group can be active at a time. These are both children of the GtkToggleButton widget, which is itself a child of the GtkButton widget we have already used several times; a toggle button is a button which can be in either a selected or an unselected condition.

Check buttons

Check buttons are the simpler of the two, so we'll look at those first. A GtkCheckButton is a box which can either be empty or have a tick mark in it; clicking on it toggles it between those two states. Creating one is as easy as:

```
GtkWidget *chk = gtk_check_button_new_with_label ("My check");
```

This creates a check button and a label to its left with the supplied text in it. (There is also a function **gtk_check_button_new**, which creates just the check box without the label – this makes things tidier if you have a label for it somewhere else in your window.) Try replacing **btn2** in the previous example with a check button like **chk** – it should look like this:

▲ A GtkCheckButton at the top-right of the window

By default, a check button which has just been created is in the unchecked state. To check the button, you call:

```
gtk_toggle_button_set_active (GTK_TOGGLE_BUTTON (chk), TRUE);
```

Setting the button's active state to **TRUE** checks the box; setting it to **FALSE** unchecks it.

There is a corresponding function to read the active state of a toggle button – to read whether a check button is currently checked into a variable, do:

```
int state = gtk_toggle_button_get_active (GTK_TOGGLE_BUTTON (chk));
```

The value of **state** will be **1** if the button is checked, or **0** otherwise.

You can also connect a handler to the **toggled** signal of a check button with **g_signal_connect** – this is equivalent to connecting to the **clicked** signal of a regular GtkButton, as we have seen in previous examples:

```
g_signal_connect (chk, "toggled", G_CALLBACK (check_toggle),
    NULL);
```

The handler for a **toggled** call looks like this:

```
void check_toggle (GtkWidget *wid, gpointer ptr)
{
  printf ("The state of the button is %d\n",
      gtk_toggle_button_get_active (GTK_TOGGLE_BUTTON (wid)));
}
```

Note that the first argument of any handler callback is always a pointer to the widget that generated the signal, so we check the state of the check button by calling **gtk_toggle_button_get_active** on the pointer received as the first argument to its handler.

Radio buttons

Radio buttons can be viewed as a group of check buttons, in which one and only one of each group is selected at a time – checking any button in the group automatically unchecks all other buttons in the group. These are shown as circular indicators.

The code controlling radio buttons is almost identical to that for check buttons; their active state can be set or checked with the same commands, and they generate a **toggled** signal when clicked.

The significant difference between radio button and check button code is that radio buttons need to be assigned to a group of other radio buttons; this is required so that the link between the set of buttons is established so that GTK knows which buttons need to be unchecked when another is checked.

Radio buttons are created using the function **gtk_radio_button_new_with_label** – this takes one additional parameter over **gtk_check_button_new_with_label**, which is the group to which the button belongs. When the first button in a group is created, this parameter is set to **NULL**:

```
GtkWidget *rad1 = gtk_radio_button_new_with_label (NULL,
    "Button 1");
```

When second and subsequent buttons are created, the group of the first button can be read with the function **gtk_radio_button_get_group** and passed into subsequent **gtk_radio_button_new_with_label** calls:

```
GSList *group = gtk_radio_button_get_group (
    GTK_RADIO_BUTTON (rad1));

GtkWidget *rad2 = gtk_radio_button_new_with_label (group,
    "Button 2");
```

Every button in the group needs to be associated with another button in the same group in this manner in order for the link to work correctly. (Any radio button which is not linked with a group will not function correctly; it will always be selected and clicking on it has no effect.)

Try replacing the check button and the label in the previous example with the pair of grouped radio buttons shown above – you should get something that looks like this:

▲ Two GtkRadioButtons at the top of the window

If you've linked them correctly, then when you click 'Button 2', it will be selected and 'Button 1' will be unselected, and vice versa.

Chapter 19

Combo boxes and list stores

Create combo boxes for user input and associate list stores with them

Widgets like spin buttons, radio buttons, and check buttons are useful to allow a user to make selections between small numbers of options, but sometimes we need to offer a larger number of options. A combo box is a good way of offering the user a selection of choices without taking up huge amounts of space; GTK offers two types of combo box.

Text combo boxes

The simpler kind of combo box is the GtkComboBoxText, which only allows each option to be plain text. Here's how to create one:

```
GtkWidget *comb = gtk_combo_box_text_new ();

gtk_combo_box_text_append_text (GTK_COMBO_BOX_TEXT (comb),
    "Option 1");
gtk_combo_box_text_append_text (GTK_COMBO_BOX_TEXT (comb),
    "Option 2");
gtk_combo_box_text_append_text (GTK_COMBO_BOX_TEXT (comb),
    "Option 3");

gtk_combo_box_set_active (GTK_COMBO_BOX (comb), 0);
```

The **gtk_combo_box_text_new** function creates an empty combo box, and entries can be added to it (in the order they should appear, from top to bottom) using calls to **gtk_combo_box_text_append_text**.

The final function call shown above, **gtk_combo_box_set_active**, sets the initial value of the combo box – in this case, setting it to **0** chooses the first option added to the box, 'Option 1'. Note that this is a function for the widget GtkComboBox, rather than for

GtkComboBoxText – because GtkComboBox is a parent of GtkComboBoxText, you can use the functions of the parent on the child with an appropriate cast.

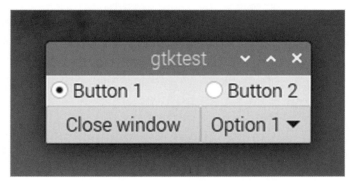

▲ A GtkComboBoxText at the bottom right of the window

To read the currently selected value, use:

```
int sel = gtk_combo_box_get_active (GTK_COMBO_BOX (comb));
```

This returns the index of the currently selected item – so 0 for 'Option 1', 1 for 'Option 2' and so on. Alternatively:

```
char *selected = gtk_combo_box_text_get_active_text (
    GTK_COMBO_BOX_TEXT (comb));
```

...can be used to return the actual text string which is selected. (Note that this function only works on text combo boxes; it can't be used on the full combo box described in the next section.)

The signal generated by a combo box when the value is changed by the user is called **changed**, so a suitable callback like:

```
void combo_changed (GtkWidget *wid, gpointer ptr)
{
    int sel = gtk_combo_box_get_active (GTK_COMBO_BOX (wid));
    char *selected = gtk_combo_box_text_get_active_text (
        GTK_COMBO_BOX_TEXT (wid));
    printf ("The value of the combo is %d %s\n", sel, selected);
}
```

...can be connected using:

```
g_signal_connect (comb, "changed", G_CALLBACK (combo_changed),
    NULL);
```

The GtkComboBoxText is a useful control for simple cases, but the full GtkComboBox gives a lot more flexibility. Like some other widgets for free-form data display, it is used as a front end on a database structure called a *list store*.

List stores

A list store can be thought of as a table of data with multiple rows and columns. Each cell of the table can store a text string, an integer, or even an image.

Once a list store is created, a combo box can be associated with it and one column of the list store can be used to provide the options for the box. The code for this is a little longer and more complex than that for a GtkComboBoxText above, but adds the potential for much more sophisticated handling of combo boxes.

Here's the code to do that:

```
int pos = 0;

GtkListStore *ls = gtk_list_store_new (1, G_TYPE_STRING);
gtk_list_store_insert_with_values (ls, NULL, pos++, 0,
    "Option 1", -1);
gtk_list_store_insert_with_values (ls, NULL, pos++, 0,
    "Option 2", -1);
gtk_list_store_insert_with_values (ls, NULL, pos++, 0,
    "Option 3", -1);

GtkWidget *comb = gtk_combo_box_new_with_model (
    GTK_TREE_MODEL (ls));

GtkCellRenderer *rend = gtk_cell_renderer_text_new ();

gtk_cell_layout_pack_start (GTK_CELL_LAYOUT (comb), rend, FALSE);
gtk_cell_layout_add_attribute (GTK_CELL_LAYOUT (comb), rend,
    "text", 0);
```

First, we create a GtkListStore:

```
GtkListStore *ls = gtk_list_store_new (1, G_TYPE_STRING);
```

The **gtk_list_store_new** function takes a list of arguments – the first is the number of columns in the list store, and this is followed by a list of the types of data stored in each column. In this example we are creating a store with a single column, and that column will hold a text string.

We then add some entries to the list store:

```
gtk_list_store_insert_with_values (ls, NULL, pos++, 0,
    "Option 1", -1);
gtk_list_store_insert_with_values (ls, NULL, pos++, 0,
    "Option 2", -1);
gtk_list_store_insert_with_values (ls, NULL, pos++, 0,
    "Option 3", -1);
```

Each call to **gtk_list_store_insert_with_values** takes the list store as an argument, followed by a **NULL** pointer. In some cases, this would be a pointer to what is called an *iterator*, which is a reference to the entry just added – we don't need this functionality, so we just set the pointer to **NULL**.

These are followed by the index within the list store where the new entry is to be placed – effectively the number of the row to be used for the data – and then a list of paired values. The first value of each pair is the column where the data is to be stored, and the second is the data itself; the list of pairs is terminated with a **-1** for the column value. In this case, we are only adding a single text string item to each row, in column 0.

We then associate a combo box with the list store:

```
GtkWidget *comb = gtk_combo_box_new_with_model (
    GTK_TREE_MODEL (ls));
```

This creates a new combo box and tells GTK that the data for this combo box comes from the **ls** list store we previously created. The data used by a combo box is of type GtkTreeModel, so we cast our list store to this type.

Now we set which column of the list store should be shown in the combo box – be warned, this gets a bit complicated!

```
GtkCellRenderer *rend = gtk_cell_renderer_text_new ();
```

First we create a GtkCellRenderer – this is a code object which is used to create a graphical representation of data in a table. In this case, it is a text renderer, which is used to display text strings.

```
gtk_cell_layout_pack_start (GTK_CELL_LAYOUT (comb), rend, FALSE);
```

We then add the renderer we just created to the cell layout of the combo box – this means that the renderer will be called when the combo box wants to display some data. (The final parameter, set to **FALSE**, is whether or not the data is expanded to fill free space in the layout; this has no effect on a combo box.)

```
gtk_cell_layout_add_attribute (GTK_CELL_LAYOUT (comb), rend,
        "text", 0);
```

Finally, we set the **text** attribute of the cell renderer to the data from the supplied column number of the list store – this causes the renderer to display the data in column 0 as text in the combo box.

Try building and running the code, and satisfy yourself that it does the same thing as the previous example with GtkComboBoxText.

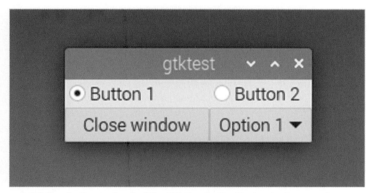

▲ A GtkComboBox instead of the GtkComboBoxText – don't worry; they are supposed to look the same!

Some of the code above probably looks a bit like black magic, and in truth it is a complicated way to put some text in a combo box; cell renderers make more sense in some other circumstances, which we will look at in the next chapter. But they are a necessary complication to using list stores to provide data for combo boxes, and that can be very useful, because we can process the data in a list store and have the combo box automatically reflect that processing.

For example, in the code above, we have put the three text strings into the list store in alphabetical order, but in the real world we can't guarantee that data will arrive in a nice tidy order like that. With a list store, it is easy to sort the data, by replacing the line:

```
GtkWidget *comb = gtk_combo_box_new_with_model (
        GTK_TREE_MODEL (ls));
```

...with:

```
GtkTreeModelSort *sorted = GTK_TREE_MODEL_SORT (
    gtk_tree_model_sort_new_with_model (GTK_TREE_MODEL (ls)));

gtk_tree_sortable_set_sort_column_id (
    GTK_TREE_SORTABLE (sorted), 0, GTK_SORT_ASCENDING);

GtkWidget *comb = gtk_combo_box_new_with_model (
    GTK_TREE_MODEL (sorted));
```

In this case, we create a GtkTreeModelSort, and initialise it with the data from our original list store. We then sort the data alphabetically by setting the sort column of the GtkTreeModelSort to 0 (because column 0 contains the data we want to sort on) and specifying ascending (from A to Z) sort order. Finally, we use the sorted model as the data source for our combo box, rather than the original unsorted model.

Similar functions exist to allow you to filter the rows in a list store, and you can combine sorts and filters to easily customise what is shown in a combo box based on settings elsewhere in an application – this is particularly useful when, for example, using a cascading series of combo boxes, each of which restricts the options in a subsequent box.

Chapter 20
Tree views

Use the GtkTreeView widget to display
information and user input options

As mentioned in the previous chapter, using a list store for a combo box can sometimes be overkill – although in some circumstances, it is exactly the right thing to do! But the situation for which a list store is really designed is as the data store for a widget called a GtkTreeView.

A GtkTreeView is a table of data arranged in columns. The table can show images as well as text, and can even contain other widgets, such as check buttons, alongside the data.

Creating a tree view

To demonstrate this, we're going to create a new list store with two entries per row, a text string and an icon. Here's the code to do that:

```
void main (int argc, char *argv[])
{
  gtk_init (&argc, &argv);

  GtkWidget *win = gtk_window_new (GTK_WINDOW_TOPLEVEL);
  GtkWidget *btn = gtk_button_new_with_label ("Close window");
  g_signal_connect (btn, "clicked", G_CALLBACK (end_program),
      NULL);
  g_signal_connect (win, "delete_event", G_CALLBACK (end_program),
      NULL);

  int pos = 0;

  GtkListStore *ls = gtk_list_store_new (2, G_TYPE_STRING,
      GDK_TYPE_PIXBUF);
  GdkPixbuf *icon = gtk_icon_theme_load_icon (
      gtk_icon_theme_get_default (), "dialog-ok-apply", 32, 0, NULL);
```

```
gtk_list_store_insert_with_values (ls, NULL, pos++, 0,
    "Option 1", 1, icon, -1);
gtk_list_store_insert_with_values (ls, NULL, pos++, 0,
    "Option 2", 1, icon, -1);
gtk_list_store_insert_with_values (ls, NULL, pos++, 0,
    "Option 3", 1, icon, -1);

GtkWidget *tv = gtk_tree_view_new_with_model (
    GTK_TREE_MODEL (ls));

GtkCellRenderer *prend = gtk_cell_renderer_pixbuf_new ();
GtkCellRenderer *trend = gtk_cell_renderer_text_new ();

gtk_tree_view_insert_column_with_attributes (
    GTK_TREE_VIEW (tv), -1, "Icon", prend, "pixbuf", 1, NULL);
gtk_tree_view_insert_column_with_attributes (
    GTK_TREE_VIEW (tv), -1, "Option", trend, "text", 0, NULL);

GtkWidget *grd = gtk_grid_new ();
gtk_grid_attach (GTK_GRID (grd), tv, 0, 0, 1, 1);
gtk_grid_attach (GTK_GRID (grd), btn, 0, 1, 1, 1);
gtk_container_add (GTK_CONTAINER (win), grd);
gtk_widget_show_all (win);
gtk_main ();
}
```

First, we call **gtk_list_store_new** to create a 2-column list store; column 0 contains a text string, as in the previous chapter, while column 1 contains a *pixbuf* (short for 'pixel buffer'), which is used to store an image.

```
GtkListStore *ls = gtk_list_store_new (2, G_TYPE_STRING,
    GDK_TYPE_PIXBUF);
```

We then create a GdkPixbuf with a small image in it – in this case, we load an icon from the current icon theme into it, but a GdkPixbuf can store any sort of image you choose to display.

```
GdkPixbuf *icon = gtk_icon_theme_load_icon (
    gtk_icon_theme_get_default (), "dialog-ok-apply", 32, 0,
    NULL);
```

We add three rows to the list store – in each case, we put a text string into column 0 of the row, and the pixbuf we created into column 1.

```
gtk_list_store_insert_with_values (ls, NULL, pos++, 0, "Option 1",
    1, icon, -1);
gtk_list_store_insert_with_values (ls, NULL, pos++, 0, "Option 2",
    1, icon, -1);
gtk_list_store_insert_with_values (ls, NULL, pos++, 0, "Option 3",
    1, icon, -1);
```

We now need to create a GtkTreeView to display the list store. The first step of this is similar to the creation of a GtkComboBox in the previous chapter – we associate the new GtkTreeView with the GtkListStore we just created.

```
GtkWidget *tv = gtk_tree_view_new_with_model (
    GTK_TREE_MODEL (ls));
```

As with the combo box, we need to create cell renderers for all the types of data we want to display; in this case, we have two – a text renderer and a pixbuf renderer.

```
GtkCellRenderer *prend = gtk_cell_renderer_pixbuf_new ();
GtkCellRenderer *trend = gtk_cell_renderer_text_new ();
```

Finally, we insert the columns we want to see into the tree view.

```
gtk_tree_view_insert_column_with_attributes (
    GTK_TREE_VIEW (tv), -1, "Icon", prend, "pixbuf", 1, NULL);
gtk_tree_view_insert_column_with_attributes (
    GTK_TREE_VIEW (tv), -1, "Option", trend, "text", 0, NULL);
```

Each call to **gtk_tree_view_insert_column_with_attributes** takes the tree view itself as the first argument. The second argument is the position of the column – this can either be the actual position, numbered from 0 at the left-hand side of the table, or as here, -1, which indicates that the column should be added as the next column; that is to the right of the rightmost column already in the table. The next parameter is the title for the column (which can be shown at the top of the table), and then the renderer we've created to be used for the column.

The final arguments are passed to the cell renderer itself, and set an attribute of the renderer to the data in a certain column of the list store – in the first instance we set the **pixbuf** attribute of the pixbuf renderer to the data in column 1, and in the second we set the **text** attribute of the text renderer to the data in column 0. (Because it is possible to set multiple attributes on some renderers, the final argument is a **NULL**, to indicate that there are no more attributes to set.)

Build and run the code, and see what happens – you should see something like this:

▲ A GtkTreeView with two columns – a pixbuf and some text

Getting input from a tree view

A tree view is useful as a display of information, but it can also be used to read user selections. If you click on one of the rows in the table, it will be highlighted – you can also move the highlight up and down through the table with the arrow keys on the keyboard.

Whenever the selected row is changed, the **cursor-changed** signal is generated by the tree view, so this can be used to call an appropriate callback:

```
g_signal_connect (tv, "cursor-changed", G_CALLBACK
    (row_selected), NULL);
```

The callback should be as follows:

```
void row_selected (GtkWidget *wid, gpointer ptr)
{
  GtkTreeSelection *sel;
  GtkTreeModel *model;
  GtkTreeIter iter;
  char *option;

  sel = gtk_tree_view_get_selection (GTK_TREE_VIEW (wid));
  if (gtk_tree_selection_get_selected (sel, &model, &iter))
  {
      gtk_tree_model_get (model, &iter, 0, &option, -1);
      printf ("The selected row contains the text %s\n", option);
  }
}
```

Finding out which row is selected requires an *iterator*, which is a data structure which stores the location of a row in a list store.

First we need to get the GtkTreeSelection for the tree view – this stores which row (or rows) are currently highlighted.

```
sel = gtk_tree_view_get_selection (GTK_TREE_VIEW (tv));
```

From a GtkTreeSelection, we then get the GtkTreeIter and GtkTreeModel associated with it. The tree model is the list store which is providing the data for the tree view, and the iterator is the actual row selected.

```
if (gtk_tree_selection_get_selected (sel, &model, &iter))
```

(This function returns **FALSE** if there is no valid selection – it's important to check for this as otherwise the next line will cause a crash if no row is selected.)

Finally, we can get the actual values from the model and iterator.

```
gtk_tree_model_get (model, &iter, 0, &option, -1);
```

As when setting a value in a list store, the arguments to this function, after the model and iterator, are a list of paired values, the first of each pair being the column to be read, and the second being a pointer to which the data should be written. Multiple values can be read from the same row with a single call, so **-1** is used for the column value of the final entry in the list, to show there are no more values to read.

In this case, a pointer to the text in the first column of the selected row is returned as **option**.

Chapter 21
Menus

Create menu bars with drop-down
menus, and also pop-up menus

Many applications have a menu bar at the top of the main window. GTK provides a number of widgets which can be used to create either menu bars or pop-up menus.

The building block of menus is the GtkMenuItem widget. Each entry in a menu is a GtkMenuItem, which has a text label associated with it. A GtkMenu widget is used to hold one or more GtkMenuItem widgets, creating a single menu of the sort seen as a pop-up or when an item on an application menu bar is selected.

Menu bars

A GtkMenuBar can be displayed at the top of an application's window; this contains a number of GtkMenuItems, each of which provides the name for a GtkMenu, as described above.

It can be slightly confusing to consider that a GtkMenuItem is both a member of a menu and the name of the entire menu, but hopefully an example will make things a bit clearer. Here's the code for an application with a menu bar:

```
void main (int argc, char *argv[])
{
  gtk_init (&argc, &argv);

  GtkWidget *win = gtk_window_new (GTK_WINDOW_TOPLEVEL);
  GtkWidget *btn = gtk_button_new_with_label ("Close window");
  g_signal_connect (btn, "clicked", G_CALLBACK (end_program),
      NULL);
  g_signal_connect (win, "delete_event", G_CALLBACK (end_program),
      NULL);

  GtkWidget *mbar = gtk_menu_bar_new ();
  GtkWidget *vbox = gtk_box_new (GTK_ORIENTATION_VERTICAL, 5);
  gtk_box_pack_start (GTK_BOX (vbox), mbar, TRUE, TRUE, 0);
  gtk_container_add (GTK_CONTAINER (win), vbox);
```

```
    GtkWidget *file_mi = gtk_menu_item_new_with_label ("File");
    gtk_menu_shell_append (GTK_MENU_SHELL (mbar), file_mi);

    GtkWidget *f_menu = gtk_menu_new ();
    gtk_menu_item_set_submenu (GTK_MENU_ITEM (file_mi), f_menu);

    GtkWidget *quit_mi = gtk_menu_item_new_with_label ("Quit");
    gtk_menu_shell_append (GTK_MENU_SHELL (f_menu), quit_mi);
    g_signal_connect (quit_mi, "activate", G_CALLBACK (end_program),
        NULL);

    gtk_box_pack_start (GTK_BOX (vbox), btn, TRUE, TRUE, 0);
    gtk_widget_show_all (win);
    gtk_main ();
}
```

First, we create a menu bar to hold the application menus.

```
    GtkWidget *mbar = gtk_menu_bar_new ();
```

We need to add it to the window; as with any other widget, to put it at the top of the window, we need to create a vertical box, pack the menu bar at the top and the rest of the window contents beneath it, and then put the vertical box into the window's container.

```
    GtkWidget *vbox = gtk_box_new (GTK_ORIENTATION_VERTICAL, 5);
    gtk_box_pack_start (GTK_BOX (vbox), mbar, TRUE, TRUE, 0);
    gtk_container_add (GTK_CONTAINER (win), vbox);
```

We then create a menu item to hold the 'File' menu, and add it to the menu bar using **gtk_menu_shell_append** – a *menu shell* is anything which can hold menu items; in practical terms, this is either a menu or a menu bar.

```
    GtkWidget *file_mi = gtk_menu_item_new_with_label ("File");
    gtk_menu_shell_append (GTK_MENU_SHELL (mbar), file_mi);
```

At this point we have a menu bar with the single item 'File' on it – we now need to create a menu to associate with the menu item.

```
    GtkWidget *f_menu = gtk_menu_new ();
```

Having created the menu, we use **gtk_menu_item_set_submenu** to set it as a submenu of the 'File' menu item.

```
gtk_menu_item_set_submenu (GTK_MENU_ITEM (file_mi), f_menu);
```

At this point, we have a menu bar with the 'File' item on it, and an empty menu as the submenu of that menu item. We now create a menu item to hold the 'Quit' option, and we use **gtk_menu_shell_append** to add this to the 'File' menu.

```
GtkWidget *quit_mi = gtk_menu_item_new_with_label ("Quit");
gtk_menu_shell_append (GTK_MENU_SHELL (f_menu), quit_mi);
```

We now have a menu bar with a single menu ('File'), which contains a single option ('Quit'), but as yet that option doesn't do anything. To make the menu item do something, we connect a handler callback to its **activate** signal with **g_signal_connect**, just as with a button.

The code to connect our existing **end_program** handler to the 'Quit' menu item is:

```
g_signal_connect (quit_mi, "activate", G_CALLBACK (end_program),
    NULL);
```

That's it – you now have a working 'Quit' menu option in your application. You can use the same process to add as many menus and menu items as you want to a menu bar.

▲ A GtkMenuBar with a single GtkMenu ('File'), which contains a single GtkMenuItem ('Quit')

Note that the function we used to add a menu to the item in the menu bar was called **gtk_menu_item_set_submenu** – effectively, the menu is regarded as a submenu of the top-level menu item in the menu bar. You can use exactly the same function to create an actual submenu from a menu item in a menu, and can nest these calls as deeply as you want to create the sort of hierarchical menu structure that more complex applications use. (From a usability point of view, it's wise to stick to no more than one additional level of submenu – having a menu create a submenu from some items is fine, but if you are creating even more submenus from the submenus themselves, the users may get confused!)

Pop-up menus

The menu bar is the most common way of adding a menu to an application, but it is also possible to use very similar code to add pop-up menus that are produced when you click buttons, tree views, or various other widgets.

Create the following handler, and connect it to the **clicked** signal on a button.

```
void button_popup (GtkWidget *wid, gpointer ptr)
{
  GtkWidget *f_menu = gtk_menu_new ();
  GtkWidget *quit_mi = gtk_menu_item_new_with_label ("Quit");
  gtk_menu_shell_append (GTK_MENU_SHELL (f_menu), quit_mi);
  g_signal_connect (quit_mi, "activate", G_CALLBACK (end_program),
      NULL);

  gtk_widget_show_all (f_menu);
  gtk_menu_popup_at_pointer (GTK_MENU (f_menu),
      gtk_get_current_event ());
}
```

This creates a menu with the single item 'Quit', as before, but instead of putting it into a menu bar, it uses the **gtk_menu_popup_at_pointer** function to display it at the mouse cursor position. When you press the button to which this handler is connected, the menu will be displayed over the button, and it can then be selected from there.

▴ A pop-up menu, launched from a button

The **gtk_menu_popup_at_pointer function** takes two arguments: the menu to be popped-up, and the system event which triggered the pop-up – in this case, the mouse click on the button, accessed by calling **gtk_get_current_event**.

This example shows a pop-up being generated by a button press, but it can also be linked to mouse events on many other widgets.

Chapter 22
Dialogs

Give users information and ask them
questions using dialogs

f we want to ask the user a question, or to inform them of something, the best way to do this is with a dialog box. GTK makes it easy to create dialogs – a GtkDialog can contain any GTK widgets, so can be as simple or as complex as you need.

The characteristic which distinguishes a dialog from a window in GTK is that a dialog interrupts the operation of the application – once a dialog is shown, the rest of the application waits until the dialog is closed.

Dialogs all have one or more buttons (typically with functions like 'OK' and 'Cancel') in what is called the *action area* at the bottom of the dialog; these close the dialog and return control to the main window. Each button in the action area generates a different return code, which is passed back from the dialog to give the user's response.

Here's the code for a simple dialog – connect this to the **clicked** signal on a button with **g_signal_connect**, and pass a pointer to the main window of your application as the general-purpose pointer in the **g_signal_connect** function:

```
void open_dialog (GtkWidget *wid, gpointer ptr)
{
  GtkWidget *dlg = gtk_dialog_new_with_buttons ("My dialog",
      GTK_WINDOW (ptr),
      GTK_DIALOG_MODAL | GTK_DIALOG_DESTROY_WITH_PARENT,
      "Cancel", 0, "OK", 1, NULL);

  int result = gtk_dialog_run (GTK_DIALOG (dlg));
  gtk_widget_destroy (dlg);
  printf ("Return code = %d\n", result);
}
```

The **gtk_dialog_new_with_buttons** function takes a number of arguments. The first is the text to be displayed on the title bar of the dialog. The second is a pointer to the main window of the application – this is why a pointer to the main window should be supplied to the **g_signal_connect** function which links this handler to a button's **clicked** signal.

The third argument is a set of flags which control the behaviour of the dialog; in this case we set it to be a *modal* dialog and set it to be destroyed along with its parent window. Making a dialog modal means that the parent window will be locked while the dialog is on display – it forces the user to close the dialog before they can continue, which is usually the desired behaviour. Making the dialog be destroyed along with its parent is just for tidiness – it means that if the main window of the application closes for some reason while the dialog is on display, then the dialog will also close. (It is quite rare to create a dialog without setting it to be modal and destroyed with its parent.)

The remaining arguments control which buttons are displayed in the action area of the dialog. This is a list of paired values; the first of each pair is the label to be displayed on a button, and the second is the return code which that button will generate when clicked. The list is terminated with a **NULL** value.

Once we have created our dialog, we call `gtk_dialog_run` – this displays the dialog and allows the user to interact with it. They will be able to operate any widgets on the dialog, but the main window will be locked while they do so, and execution of code waits inside the `gtk_dialog_run` function until a button in the action area is clicked. At this point, you need to call `gtk_widget_destroy` on the dialog to get rid of it – you might have expected clicking a button to remove the dialog, but this doesn't happen; the dialog stays on screen until it is explicitly removed.

Build and run the code – when you click the button which calls this handler, the dialog should be displayed.

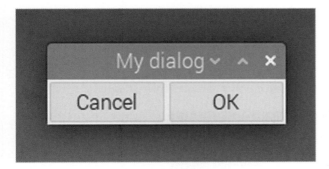

▲ A simple GtkDialog, with two buttons in the action area

While the dialog is on screen, clicking any other controls on the main window will have no effect. When you close the dialog by clicking either the 'OK' or 'Cancel' button, you will see a message showing the return code for the button you clicked in the terminal window from which you launched the application.

That's a basic dialog, but it's a bit small and bare! Let's add a label to it to ask the user a question. To do this, we have to access the dialog's *content area* – effectively, a dialog is a GtkWindow which holds a vertically oriented GtkBox with two GtkContainers in it – one is the action area at the bottom which holds the buttons, and the other is the content area at the top.

We add any additional content to the dialog in the content area, which can be accessed using the function **gtk_dialog_get_content_area**.

Modify the handler above like this:

```c
void open_dialog (GtkWidget *wid, gpointer ptr)
{
  GtkWidget *dlg = gtk_dialog_new_with_buttons ("My dialog",
      GTK_WINDOW (ptr),
      GTK_DIALOG_MODAL | GTK_DIALOG_DESTROY_WITH_PARENT,
      "Cancel", 0, "OK", 1, NULL);

  GtkWidget *lbl = gtk_label_new ("A question for the user");

  gtk_container_add (
      GTK_CONTAINER (gtk_dialog_get_content_area (GTK_DIALOG (dlg))),
      lbl);
  gtk_widget_show (lbl);

  int result = gtk_dialog_run (GTK_DIALOG (dlg));
  gtk_widget_destroy (dlg);
  printf ("Return code = %d\n", result);
}
```

We've used the familiar **gtk_container_add** function to add our label to the content area of the dialog. Note that we also needed to call **gtk_widget_show** on the label we added – **gtk_dialog_run** automatically shows the widgets which are a part of the dialog itself, like the background and the buttons, but you need to explicitly show everything else you add.

▲ A GtkDialog with a label added to the content area

As with the main application window, if we want to add more than one widget to the content area, we first need to add a box or a grid, and then to put the widgets into that.

Chapter 23
Built-in dialogs

GTK contains some ready-made dialogs for frequently used functions

Th/ere are some common dialog boxes which are used in many desktop applications; for example, for choosing a file name to load or save, or for selecting a colour. GTK includes ready-made versions of these common dialog boxes which can easily be included in an application without needing to create every aspect of the dialog from scratch.

For most of these dialogs, there is a GTK button which launches the dialog; the easiest way to include the dialog is to include the appropriate button in your application, and everything is then done for you.

File chooser dialogs

Let's look at an example of a file chooser dialog, which is used to get the name and path of a file which can then be used in a subsequent file read operation.

```
static void file_selected (GtkFileChooserButton *btn, gpointer ptr)
{
    printf ("%s selected\n", gtk_file_chooser_get_filename
        (GTK_FILE_CHOOSER (btn)));
}

void main (int argc, char *argv[])
{
    gtk_init (&argc, &argv);

    GtkWidget *win = gtk_window_new (GTK_WINDOW_TOPLEVEL);
    GtkWidget *btn = gtk_button_new_with_label ("Close window");
    g_signal_connect (btn, "clicked", G_CALLBACK (end_program),
        NULL);
    g_signal_connect (win, "delete_event", G_CALLBACK (end_program),
        NULL);

    GtkWidget *vbox = gtk_box_new (GTK_ORIENTATION_VERTICAL, 5);
```

```
    gtk_container_add (GTK_CONTAINER (win), vbox);

    GtkWidget *fc_btn = gtk_file_chooser_button_new ("Select file",
        GTK_FILE_CHOOSER_ACTION_OPEN);
    g_signal_connect (fc_btn, "file-set",
        G_CALLBACK (file_selected), NULL);

    gtk_box_pack_start (GTK_BOX (vbox), fc_btn, TRUE, TRUE, 0);
    gtk_box_pack_start (GTK_BOX (vbox), btn, TRUE, TRUE, 0);
    gtk_widget_show_all (win);
    gtk_main ();
}
```

A widget of type GtkFileChooserButton is created, and added to the window. The
gtk_file_chooser_button_new function takes two arguments; the first is the title
to apply to the file chooser window when it is opened, and the second determines what
the file chooser window will do. In this case, we want to open an existing file, so
GTK_FILE_CHOOSER_ACTION_OPEN is used. (The alternative is to select an existing folder,
for which the argument would be **GTK_FILE_CHOOSER_ACTION_SELECT_FOLDER**.)

The **file-set** signal is connected to the button – this is called when the user makes a
selection – and in the handler for that signal, the **gtk_file_chooser_get_filename**
function is called to read back the name of the file selected.

When this code is run, you will see a window which looks like this:

▲ A GtkFileChooserButton

The folder icon at the right-hand side of the top button indicates that it is a file chooser;
the title of the button is the name of the currently selected file, which is '(None)' when the
application is first run. If you click the button, a file chooser dialog will open:

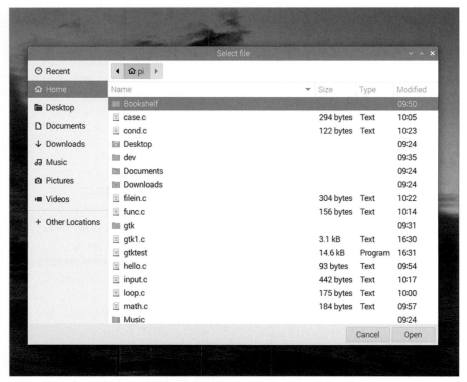

▲ The dialog opened from a GtkFileChooserButton to select an existing file

This provides a standard file browser; because we opened the window in 'file open' mode, it will only allow you to select a file that already exists on the file system. Use the browser to choose a file, and click 'Open'; when the window closes, the title of the button will update to show the selected file, and the full file path of the selected file will be printed to the terminal window from which you launched the application.

You can use a GtkFileChooserButton to open a browser which will select an existing file or folder, but the designers of GTK decided that you can't use this method to choose the location to which a new file can be saved. For that, you need to create a GtkFileChooser dialog yourself.

Modify the code above as follows:

```c
static void save_file (GtkWidget *btn, gpointer ptr)
{
    GtkWidget *sch = gtk_file_chooser_dialog_new ("Save file",
        GTK_WINDOW (ptr), GTK_FILE_CHOOSER_ACTION_SAVE,
        "Cancel", 0, "OK", 1, NULL);
    if (gtk_dialog_run (GTK_DIALOG (sch)) == 1)
    {
```

```
    printf ("%s selected\n", gtk_file_chooser_get_filename
        (GTK_FILE_CHOOSER (sch)));
  }
  gtk_widget_destroy (sch);
}

void main (int argc, char *argv[])
{
  gtk_init (&argc, &argv);

  GtkWidget *win = gtk_window_new (GTK_WINDOW_TOPLEVEL);
  GtkWidget *btn = gtk_button_new_with_label ("Close window");
  g_signal_connect (btn, "clicked", G_CALLBACK (end_program),
      NULL);
  g_signal_connect (win, "delete_event", G_CALLBACK (end_program),
      NULL);

  GtkWidget *vbox = gtk_box_new (GTK_ORIENTATION_VERTICAL, 5);
  gtk_container_add (GTK_CONTAINER (win), vbox);

  GtkWidget *fc_btn = gtk_button_new_with_label ("Save file");
  g_signal_connect (fc_btn, "clicked", G_CALLBACK (save_file), win);

  gtk_box_pack_start (GTK_BOX (vbox), fc_btn, TRUE, TRUE, 0);
  gtk_box_pack_start (GTK_BOX (vbox), btn, TRUE, TRUE, 0);
  gtk_widget_show_all (win);
  gtk_main ();
}
```

In this case, we create a button to open the dialog, and then have to manually create and open the dialog in the button handler.

The dialog is created by calling **gtk_file_chooser_dialog_new**, whose arguments are very similar to those for **gtk_dialog_new_with_buttons** that we saw in the previous chapter. First, the title of the dialog is provided, followed by a pointer to the parent window and then a flag which determines the behaviour of the dialog – in this case, it is set up to provide a file name and path to which a file can be saved. The remaining arguments are a **NULL**-terminated list of pairs of labels and return values for the buttons at the bottom of the dialog.

We create the dialog and call **gtk_dialog_run** when the button is pressed; the button handler then waits for the dialog to return. We then read the file path back from the file chooser using **gtk_file_chooser_get_filename**, as we did for the file open dialog.

If you run this code and press the 'Save file' button, you'll see that a file save chooser is slightly different from a file open chooser, in that it has a box to allow a new file name to be entered:

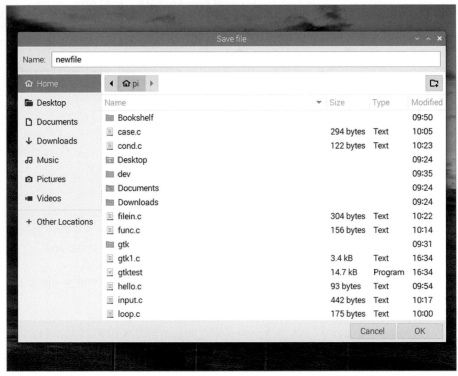

▲ A GtkFileChooserDialog to select a file to be saved

Enter a new file name and select a location for the new file; when you press 'OK', the path to the new file will be printed to the terminal.

There are several other predefined dialogs which can be added to an application just by including a button. Two of the more useful ones are the colour picker and the font chooser.

Colour picker

Sometimes you need to allow the user to select a colour – to determine how things will be highlighted, for example. This is easy to do with the GtkColorButton. (Note that whenever GTK refers to 'colour', it does so using the US spelling, without the 'u' – it's a common source of compile-time errors for those of us on the east side of the Atlantic!)

Colours in GTK are stored as GdkRGBA data structures, which contain separate values for the red, green, and blue components of a colour. The GtkColorButton therefore operates on data stored as a GdkRGBA.

Here's an example of using a GtkColorButton:

```c
static void col_selected (GtkColorChooser *btn, gpointer ptr)
{
  GdkRGBA col;
  gtk_color_chooser_get_rgba (btn, &col);
  printf ("red = %f; green = %f; blue = %f\n", col.red, col.green,
      col.blue);
}

void main (int argc, char *argv[])
{
  gtk_init (&argc, &argv);

  GtkWidget *win = gtk_window_new (GTK_WINDOW_TOPLEVEL);
  GtkWidget *btn = gtk_button_new_with_label ("Close window");
  g_signal_connect (btn, "clicked", G_CALLBACK (end_program),
      NULL);
  g_signal_connect (win, "delete_event", G_CALLBACK (end_program),
      NULL);

  GtkWidget *vbox = gtk_box_new (GTK_ORIENTATION_VERTICAL, 5);
  gtk_container_add (GTK_CONTAINER (win), vbox);

  GtkWidget *col_btn = gtk_color_button_new ();
  g_signal_connect (col_btn, "color-set", G_CALLBACK (col_selected),
      NULL);

  gtk_box_pack_start (GTK_BOX (vbox), col_btn, TRUE, TRUE, 0);
  gtk_box_pack_start (GTK_BOX (vbox), btn, TRUE, TRUE, 0);
  gtk_widget_show_all (win);
  gtk_main ();
}
```

We create the colour picker button in the same way as the file chooser button, and we connect to the **color-set** signal on it to detect when the user has made a selection. The handler for this signal calls **gtk_color_chooser_get_rgba** to read the selected value back into a GdkRGBA structure, and then prints out the red, green, and blue values.

If you run this, you'll see that the colour button shows a small rectangle of the currently selected colour:

▲ A GtkColorButton

When clicked, the colour picker dialog is shown, which allows a colour to be selected from the palette of standard colours, or allows a custom colour to be created by pressing the '+' button.

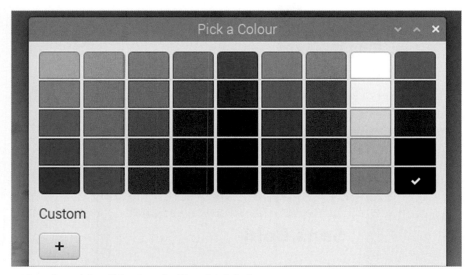

▲ The colour picker dialog launched by a GtkColorButton

When you click 'OK', the selected red, green, and blue values will be printed to the terminal.

Font selector

Another common operation is to select a font; this is used in many office applications, for example. GTK provides a font selector which works in the same way as the colour picker.

Just change the GtkColorButton in the example above for a GtkFontButton:

```
GtkWidget *fnt_btn = gtk_font_button_new ();
g_signal_connect (fnt_btn, "font-set", G_CALLBACK (fnt_selected),
    NULL);
```

And create the handler for the **font-set** signal:

```
static void fnt_selected (GtkFontChooser *btn, gpointer ptr)
{
   printf ("font = %s\n", gtk_font_chooser_get_font (btn));
}
```

When run, a font button is shown with the currently selected font name:

▲ A GtkFontButton

Pressing the font button opens the selector dialog, which allows you to pick any of the fonts currently installed on the system:

▲ The font selector dialog launched by a GtkFontButton

When you click 'OK', the selected font name and size will be printed to the terminal.

Chapter 24
Customising widgets

Change the properties of widgets
to alter how they look

n all the examples we've seen so far, we have used widgets in their default state; we've just created the widget with the **gtk_<widget name>_new** function call and used it. However, GTK does allow a degree of customisation of widgets by setting the *properties* for each.

As an example, we are going to look at some of the properties of the basic GtkButton widget. Try this example:

```
void main (int argc, char *argv[])
{
  gtk_init (&argc, &argv);

  GtkWidget *win = gtk_window_new (GTK_WINDOW_TOPLEVEL);
  GtkWidget *btn = gtk_button_new_with_label ("Close window");
  g_signal_connect (btn, "clicked", G_CALLBACK (end_program),
      NULL);
   g_signal_connect (win, "delete_event", G_CALLBACK (end_program),
      NULL);

  GtkWidget *btn2 = gtk_button_new_with_label ("My button");
  g_object_set (G_OBJECT (btn2), "relief", GTK_RELIEF_NONE, NULL);

  GtkWidget *box = gtk_box_new (GTK_ORIENTATION_VERTICAL, 5);
  gtk_box_pack_start (GTK_BOX (box), btn2, TRUE, TRUE, 0);
  gtk_box_pack_start (GTK_BOX (box), btn, TRUE, TRUE, 0);
  gtk_container_add (GTK_CONTAINER (win), box);
  gtk_widget_show_all (win);
  gtk_main ();
}
```

This is familiar code from previous examples, but the highlighted line is new.

g_object_set takes as arguments the name of a widget, followed by a **NULL**-terminated list of property names and property values. In this case, we are setting the **relief** property of the GtkButton **btn2** to **GTK_RELIEF_NONE**.

The 'relief' of a GtkButton controls how the border looks. The borders of some GTK widgets have a degree of shading applied around them to provide a 3D appearance – by default, a GtkButton has this shading applied, which makes the button appear to stand out slightly from the window background. By setting the relief to **GTK_RELIEF_NONE**, this 3D shading is removed – if you run the program above, you should be able to clearly see the difference between the two buttons on the window. (You can use the **TAB** key to move the dotted outline between the buttons to show the difference more clearly.)

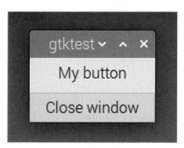

▲ A GtkButton with the `relief` property set to GTK_RELIEF_NONE

Here's another example. Remove the setting of the **relief** property, and change the name of the button by adding an underscore:

```
GtkWidget *btn2 = gtk_button_new_with_label ("My_button");
```

You should end up with a button that looks like this:

▲ A GtkButton with an underline in the label and the `use-underline` property set to FALSE

If you now set the **use-underline** property:

```
g_object_set (G_OBJECT (btn2), "use-underline", TRUE, NULL);
```

...the underscore will vanish, but will reappear under the 'b' of 'button' if you hold down the **ALT** key on the keyboard:

▲ The same GtkButton, but with `use-underline` set to TRUE

All widgets have properties that can be set like this. As another example, try replacing the GtkButton with a GtkLabel:

```
GtkWidget *lbl = gtk_label_new ("My label");
```

...and then setting the **angle** property of the label to 45 degrees:

```
g_object_set (G_OBJECT (lbl), "angle", 45.0, NULL);
```

(Note that it is important to enter the angle as 45.0, rather than just as 45 – the value expected is a floating-point number, and adding the .0 to the end of the value ensures that the compiler treats it as such.)

You should end up with a window which looks like this, with the label text at a 45-degree angle to the horizontal:

▲ A GtkLabel with the `angle` property set to 45.0

In many cases, widgets also have dedicated functions to set each property which can be used instead of the generic **g_object_set** function (in the examples above, **gtk_button_set_relief**, **gtk_button_set_use_underline**, and **gtk_label_set_angle**, respectively). The advantage of **g_object_set** is that it can be used to set multiple properties in one line, which can shorten your code significantly.

The GTK online documentation page for each widget lists all the properties and dedicated functions to set their values. For the two examples above, this can be found at

https://docs.gtk.org/gtk3/class.Button.html and **https://docs.gtk.org/gtk3/class.Label.html** –
it's worth having a look through the options for any widget you want to use. (These pages are
also a good way of finding out what signals are generated by a widget when a user interacts
with it.)

An introduction to themes

The other way that GTK widgets can be customised is by the use of a *theme*. A theme
affects the appearance of every instance of a widget in every GTK application, rather
than changing the appearance of individual widgets one at a time. There is a selection of
themes installed in Raspberry Pi OS (and in most other Linux desktop distributions), in the
directory **/usr/share/themes**.
This directory contains a number of named folders, each of which is a theme for either GTK or
other themeable applications. If a named folder contains a subfolder named **gtk-3.0**, then the
name of that folder is also a valid GTK 3 theme name.

Which of the themes is currently used by GTK applications is usually controlled by the
xsettings daemon, a process which runs in the background and provides configuration
information to all desktop applications. On Raspberry Pi OS, to change which theme is set in the
daemon, you need to change a value in a configuration file.

To do this, check to see if there is a file called **desktop.conf** in the directory
~/.config/lxsession/LXDE-pi. If there isn't, create one by copying the file
/etc/xdg/lxsession/LXDE-pi/desktop.conf into that directory.

If you then look in the **desktop.conf** file with a text editor, there is a section headed **[GTK]**.
Somewhere under this heading is a line starting **sNet/ThemeName=**, which by default on
Raspberry Pi OS is set to **PiXflat**. If you change **PiXflat** in this line to the name of another
GTK 3 theme (any directory in **/usr/share/themes** which includes a **gtk-3.0** subdirectory), the
theme in use will automatically update and you should see every GTK application running redraw
with the new theme.

Creating a theme is not for the faint-hearted, but if you are interested, look inside one of the
gtk-3.0 subdirectories in the directory **/usr/share/themes**.

The theme is contained within the file named **gtk.css**, which is a CSS (cascading style sheet)
file, similar to those used to apply styles to web pages. Due to the complexity of most themes,
this file quite often calls in other .css files from the theme folder with @import statements.

The theme .css files are plain text and can be opened in your editor of choice. Each contains
styling information for all the widgets which the theme customises – each widget is listed with a
number of states in which it can appear, and the various parameters controlling how the widget
is displayed can be modified.

If you want to play with themes, make sure you take a backup of the files in the theme
directory before you change anything. The safest thing to do is to copy the entire theme folder
and give it a new name, set the **ThemeName** in **desktop.conf** to the name of your new theme,
and then you can modify the .css files in your new folder to your heart's content!

Chapter 25
Glade

Use this layout editor to more easily create
window layouts for applications

A s can be seen in the previous chapters, while creating widgets with GTK is a lot easier than doing it all from scratch by writing pixels to screen buffers, you can still end up with quite a lot of code for even a fairly simple window layout, and you do have to think quite carefully about the code you are writing to make sure the window looks the way you want it to. It's also less than ideal that you can't actually see what the window will look like until you run the application.

Fortunately, there is a way to work on the layout of a window without having to write all its code, and that is to use a *layout editor*. GTK allows the layout of widgets on a window to be defined in an XML file, which is then loaded and drawn on the screen when the application runs – you still need to link up the behaviour of any widgets to code, but the appearance of the widgets can be determined in advance. A layout editor is a useful tool to create such an XML file.

The most widely used layout editor for GTK is a tool called Glade. There are two versions of Glade, one for GTK 2 applications and one for GTK 3 applications; they aren't interchangeable, so you need to use the correct one. The version to create GTK 3 applications is called 'glade'. And, just to be perverse, the version you need to create GTK 2 applications is called 'glade-3'. (Yes, that is counter-intuitive and quite annoying!)

The first thing we need to do is to install glade. At a terminal, type **sudo apt-get install glade**, and answer yes to any prompts. You should then have an entry labelled 'Glade' in the Programming section of the main menu. Launch it, and then click the new project button – the rectangle with a plus sign at the top left – you should then see a screen like the one shown overleaf.

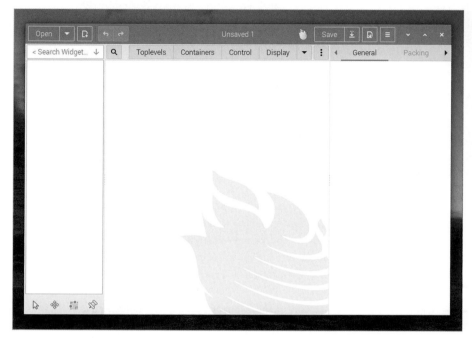

▲ The Glade layout editor

This is the basic design screen in Glade. The column on the left is a hierarchical list of all the widgets in your design – this is blank to start with. The centre part of the window is where you can see the actual layout of your design, and the column at the right allows you to set the properties for each widget.

Using Glade to create a layout file

We'll create a simple window for our application, so the first thing we need to do is to add a top-level window. At the top of the screen, click the button labelled 'Toplevels', and then click 'GtkWindow' in the drop-down that appears – this will add a blank window in the layout area in the centre of the screen:

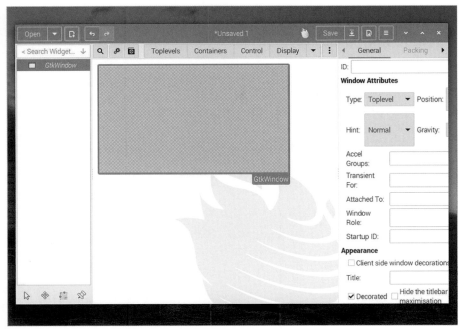

▲ An empty window

Next, let's add a Box to allow us to add some widgets. At the top of the screen, click the button labelled 'Containers' and then click 'GtkBox' in the drop-down; then move the cursor inside the blank window and click within it. A vertically oriented box will be drawn with three items, as shown overleaf.

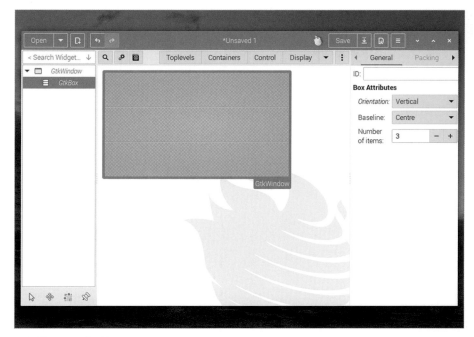

▲ Adding a vertical box

    In the widget properties browser on the right of the screen, change 'Number of items' to 2 to remove one of the items from the box. We are then going to add a label as the upper item and a button as the lower item. First, click the button labelled 'Display' at the top of the screen, then click 'GtkLabel' in the drop-down, and then place the cursor inside the upper item on the box and click to place the label. Do the same in the lower item on the box to place a button, which you can find under the button labelled 'Control' at the top of the screen. You should then have something which looks like this:

▲ With a label and a button added

If you look at the top of the right-hand column, you'll see the hierarchy of widgets being displayed – a GtkWindow, containing a GtkBox, containing a GtkLabel and a GtkButton. If you click on one of the widgets in the hierarchy, the options displayed in the tabbed area at the bottom of the right-hand column will be those for that widget.

Click on the GtkLabel, and scroll through the options on the 'General' tab; under the section labelled 'Appearance' is the entry 'Label' – use this to set the text in the label to whatever you want.

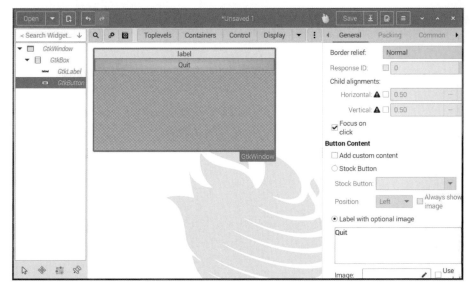

▲ The widget properties editor

Click on the GtkButton and in its properties find the section labelled 'Button Content'. In the entry 'Label with optional image', change the label for the button to 'Quit'.

It's worth investigating the options on all the tabs in the property editor on the right – there are far too many to go into here, but of particular interest are those on the 'Packing' tab; these allow you to set the expand, fill, and padding options which were available when adding widgets to boxes from code – if you play with them, you can get a good feeling for how much control you have over layout of the window, particularly when combining multiple boxes inside each other, as Glade allows you to do.

Before you can use a Glade layout, you need to assign a unique ID to each widget that you want to access from the code. These can be set in the ID box at the top of the General tab in the properties editor, and will then be displayed in the widget hierarchy on the left. So select your window, button, and label in turn, and enter an ID for each – set them to 'window1', 'button1', and 'label1', respectively. Remember these names, as they are important when linking the code to the layout file. There is one *vital* rule – every widget in a layout file must have a unique name. If two widgets have the same name, the layout file is invalid and will not load correctly.

Now click the 'Save' button at the top right of the screen, and save your layout as **mylayout.glade**. Make sure you save the file in the same directory where you are storing your GTK source code.

Using a layout file in a GTK application

Now we need to load the layout file into some GTK code. Try the following:

```
#include <gtk/gtk.h>

void main (int argc, char *argv[])
{
  gtk_init (&argc, &argv);

  GtkBuilder *builder = gtk_builder_new_from_file (
      "mylayout.glade");

  GtkWidget *win = (GtkWidget *) gtk_builder_get_object (builder,
      "window1");
  gtk_widget_show_all (win);
  gtk_main ();
}
```

The **gtk_init** and **gtk_main** calls are the same as we have seen before, but the code between them uses a GtkBuilder, a code object which reads in and processes a layout file. We create a GtkBuilder object and load the layout file into it.

```
  GtkBuilder *builder = gtk_builder_new_from_file (
      "mylayout.glade");
```

The widgets which we created in the layout file can now all be accessed by calls to **gtk_builder_get_object**, and used as before. So we get the object which was named **window1** in the layout file.

```
  GtkWidget *win = (GtkWidget *) gtk_builder_get_object (builder,
      "window1");
```

And we show it as before:

```
  gtk_widget_show_all (win);
```

If you build and run this code, our simple window should be displayed on the screen:

▲ The window created in Glade when run

As mentioned above, layout files control the appearance of a window; to make the widgets do things, we need to connect signals as before, so let's modify our code accordingly.

```
void end_program (GtkWidget *wid, gpointer ptr)
{
    gtk_main_quit ();
}

void main (int argc, char *argv[])
{
    gtk_init (&argc, &argv);

    GtkBuilder *builder = gtk_builder_new_from_file (
        "mylayout.glade");

    GtkWidget *win = (GtkWidget *) gtk_builder_get_object (builder,
        "window1");
    GtkWidget *btn = (GtkWidget *) gtk_builder_get_object (builder,
        "button1");
    g_signal_connect (btn, "clicked", G_CALLBACK (end_program), NULL);

    gtk_widget_show_all (win);
    gtk_main ();
}
```

This time, we also get the button widget from the builder and connect the **end_program** callback to it with **g_signal_connect**, as we've done before. Build and run, and this time the button should close the program.

Using layout files can make the amount of code you need to write a lot shorter, and the use of Glade makes it easier to create complex interfaces with more customisation of your widgets. For small applications with a simple window, it's probably more straightforward just to do everything in C, but for anything more complex, using a layout file can make the code a lot more readable.

Next steps

One thing which should be obvious to anyone who has worked through this book and reached this point is that GTK is a fairly huge subject! There are dozens of widgets, and hundreds of different ways they can be configured and used – any comprehensive guide to using them all would run into several hundred pages.

The best reference to GTK – and the best place to find further information if you want to do more with it – is the official developer documentation, which can be found online at **https://docs.gtk.org/gtk3/**. This gives far more detail on every aspect of GTK – the reference section listing all the functions and properties associated with each widget, which can be found under 'Classes', is particularly useful.

Hopefully this book has given you an idea of where to get started with GTK programming, and enough of a foothold to be able to experiment for yourself. Happy GUI designing!

Chapter 26
C quick reference

Make use of these handy cheat sheets and
code examples

Control Structures

If

```
if (<test>)
  <code executed if test is true>
```

If-else

```
if (<test>)
  <code executed if test is true>
else
  <code executed if test is false>
```

Multiple if-else

```
if (<test1>)
  <code executed if test1 is true>
else if (<test2>)
  <code executed if test1 is false and test2 is true>
else
  <code executed if test1 is false and test2 is false>
```

Switch

```
switch (<variable>)
{
  case <testval1> : <code executed if variable is testval1>
                    break;

  case <testval2> : <code executed if variable is testval2>
                    break;
```

```
        default :         <code executed if variable is neither testval1
                             nor testval2>
                          break;
    }
```

Switch with fall-through

```
    switch (<variable>)
    {
      case <testval1> : <code executed if variable is testval1>

      case <testval2> : <code executed if variable is either testval1
                           or testval2>
                        break;

        default :         <code executed if variable is neither testval1
                             nor testval2>
                          break;
    }
```

While

```
    while (<test>)
      <code executed repeatedly while test is true>
```

Do-while

```
    do
      <code executed once and then repeatedly while test is true>
    while (<test>);
```

For

```
    for (<initial condition>; <increment>; <termination condition>)
          <code executed repeatedly until termination condition
              is true>
```

In all loops, the keyword **break** can be used to exit the loop and resume execution immediately after the loop.

In all loops, the keyword `continue` can be used to skip code remaining in the body of the loop and resume execution at the next iteration of the loop test.

Variable Types

Name	Description	Size (bytes)
char	Single alphanumeric character	1
signed char	Signed 8-bit integer (–128 – 127)	1
unsigned char	Unsigned 8-bit integer (0 – 255)	1
short, signed short	Signed 16-bit integer (–32768 – 32767)	2
unsigned short	Unsigned 16-bit integer (0 – 65535)	2
int, signed int	Signed 32-bit integer (–2147483648 –2147483647)	4
unsigned int	Unsigned 32-bit integer (0 – 4294967295)	4
long, signed long	Signed 32-bit integer (–2147483648 – 2147483647)	4
unsigned long	Unsigned 32-bit integer (0 – 4294967295)	4
float	Floating-point value (+/– 3.402823×10^{38})	4
double	Double-precision floating-point value (+/– 10^{308})	8

Depending on platform, int can be either a short int (16 bits) or a long int (32 bits); on Raspberry Pi OS, as per the table above, int is a long (32 bits) integer value.

Format Specifiers

Specifier	Format / type
%c	Alphanumeric character / char
%d	Signed decimal value / int
%ld	Signed decimal value / long int

%u	Unsigned decimal value / int
%lu	Unsigned decimal value / long int
%o	Octal value / int
%lo	Octal value / long int
%x, %X	Hexadecimal value / int [1]
%lx, %lX	Hexadecimal value / long int [1]
%f	Floating-point value / float
%e	Exponential value / float
%s	Text string / char pointer

1. **%x** displays a value as hexadecimal with lower-case letters a through f; **%X** displays it with upper-case letters A through F.

The width (or minimum number of characters printed) can be set by inserting a number between the % and the letter; this will pad a value shorter than this with spaces at the start. To pad with spaces at the end, insert a – between the % and the number. To pad with leading zeroes, insert a **0** between the % and the number.

For example, to print an integer variable with the value 42, using the format specifier **"%5d"** will print 42 with three spaces before it. The format specifier **"%-5d"** will print 42 with three spaces after it. The format specifier **"%05d"** will print it as 00042.

The number of decimal places shown for a floating-point or exponential value can be set by inserting a decimal point followed by a number between the % and the letter; this can be combined with a width by putting the width before the decimal point.

For example, to print a floating-point variable with the value 76.54321, using the format specifier **"%.2f"** will print it as 76.54. The format specifier **"%08.2f"** will print it as 00076.54. (Note that the decimal point takes up one character of the specified width.)

Operators

The operators in the table below produce a result which can be assigned to another variable, e.g. **c** = **a** + **b**, but do not affect the values of **a** or **b**.

Symbol	Function
a + b	Addition
a - b	Subtraction
a * b	Multiplication
a / b	Division
a % b	Modulo (remainder of **a** / **b**)
a & b	Bitwise AND
a | b	Bitwise OR
a ^ b	Bitwise XOR
a << b	Bit shift left
a >> b	Bit shift right
~a	Bitwise 1's complement
!a	Logical NOT

The operators in the table below modify the value of **a** directly.

Symbol	Function
a++	Increment **a** by one [2]
a--	Decrement **a** by one [2]
++a	Increment **a** by one [2]

`--aa`	Decrement **a** by one [2]
`a += b`	Increment **a** by **b**
`a -= b`	Decrement **a** by **b**
`a *= b`	Multiply **a** by **b**
`a /= b`	Divide **a** by **b**
`a %= b`	**a** = remainder of **a** / **b**
`a &= b`	Bitwise AND **a** with **b**
`a |= b`	Bitwise OR **a** with **b**
`a ^= b`	Bitwise XOR **a** with **b**
`a <<= b`	Bit shift **a** left by **b**
`a >>= b`	Bit shift **a** right by **b**

2. The difference between **a++** and **++a** is that if they are used in a test, such as `if (a++)`, **a++** tests the value and then increments it, while **++a** increments the value first and then tests the incremented value.

The operators in the table below are used for comparisons in tests.

Symbol	Function
`==`	Is equal to
`!=`	Is not equal to
`>`	Is greater than
`<`	Is less than
`>=`	Is greater than or equal to
`<=`	Is less than or equal to

AN INTRODUCTION TO C AND GUI PROGRAMMING